**Praise for *Surviving and* ˈ
*A Handbook for Digital Le***

'Alan Brown has created a great review of the opportunities and challenges faced by executives as they look to take advantage of AI. Packed with experience and advice, this is a book for anyone looking to make a step change in their digital leadership skills as we get ready to go into the next leg of the technology journey.'

— **Christine Ashton**, CIO, UKRI

'Alan's very practical exploration of AI in the context of digital transformation is a timely guide for organizations across all sectors.'

— **David Birch**, author, advisor and commentator on digital financial services

'Based on deep experiences driving sustained organizational change, this book brings the insights you need to guide your digital strategy in the new AI era. It's an excellent handbook for busy leaders who need to understand the true potential of AI.'

— **Brigadier Stefan Crossfield**, Chief Digital and Data Officer, Principal AI Officer, British Army

'This book's insights into AI adoption will enable Digital Leaders to survive and thrive in these turbulent times.'

— **Jacqueline de Rojas CBE**, President, Digital Leaders

'A wide ranging and compelling exploration of all the key questions that the age of AI raises for business, political and public sector leaders. Professor Brown brings his massive experience of software engineering and digital transformation to AI, illuminating the gap between the potential state of the art and the likely state of the current practice and addressing the decisions that will have to be made. A personal plea to executive leaders: please read the section on data resilience!'

— **James Herbert**, CEO, Pivotl

'There are a lot of leaders out there currently daunted at the prospect of developing an AI strategy for their organization. This book is an informative, comprehensive and accessible guide to all the key issues that need to be considered when preparing to counter the threats posed and exploit the opportunities offered by this rapidly evolving technology.'

— **Tony Moretta**, CEO, Digital Jersey

'This book serves as an invaluable compass for anyone navigating the complex landscape of AI implementation. With clarity and insight, it demystifies the misconceptions surrounding AI, offering a pragmatic roadmap to define and execute AI programmes that deliver tangible value. The inclusion of real-world industry case studies not only breathes life into the concepts but also provides the inspiration and courage leaders need to confidently embark on the next phase of digitalization. A must-read for those seeking to thrive in the age of AI.'

— **Rashik Parmar MBE FBCS**, Group CEO, BCS, The Chartered Institute for IT

'This is the most compelling book on how leaders can embrace AI in their organizations that I've encountered. It will make a great handbook for senior staff in any sector as they attempt to navigate themselves and their teams through digital transformation with AI.'

— **Professor Edward Rochead**, chair of the Alliance for Data Science Professionals

'This book is a "must-read" for leaders responsible for navigating the challenges and opportunities that AI brings.'

— **Tim Vorley OBE**, Pro-Vice Chancellor and Dean, Oxford Brookes Business School

'A comprehensive view into AI's impact and directions. A book that offers the thought-provoking insights every leader needs.'

— **Dave West**, CEO and Product Owner, Scrum.org

Surviving and Thriving in the Age of AI

Surviving and Thriving in the Age of AI
A Handbook for Digital Leaders

Alan W. Brown

LONDON PUBLISHING PARTNERSHIP

Published by London Publishing Partnership
www.londonpublishingpartnership.co.uk

Published in association with
Enlightenment Economics
www.enlightenmenteconomics.com

ISBN: 978-1-916749-18-4 (pbk)
ISBN: 978-1-916749-19-1 (iPDF)
ISBN: 978-1-916749-20-7 (epub)

A catalogue record for this book is
available from the British Library

This book has been composed in Candara

Copy-edited and typeset by
T&T Productions Ltd, London
www.tandtproductions.com

Cover image: Canva

Printed and bound in Great Britain
by Hobbs the Printers Ltd

www.carbonbalancedprint.com
CBP2250

Contents

Preface

The relentless march of artificial intelligence presents both unprecedented opportunities and significant challenges for businesses and leaders across all sectors and all industries. Its potential seems unbounded. However, the constant barrage of news and conflicting opinions makes gaining a clear understanding of AI's true implications feel like an overwhelming task.

This book cuts through the noise and acts as a guide to how to survive and thrive in the age of AI. By providing an accessible collection of short, practical insights, it offers digital leaders a framework for understanding the issues and implications of AI in this time of significant digital disruption.

The book focuses on three key questions.

1. *What defines this new era of AI?* Answering this question will provide you with the context for understanding the current AI landscape and its unique characteristics.

2. *How will I need to change my thinking and behaviour in the AI era?* Exploring this topic will demonstrate the potential impact of AI on daily work and life.

3. *What steps can I take to prepare for the future directions and impact of AI?* Here we will find out how to go about asking better questions to deepen your insight, critically engage with key aspects of AI and plan for its use.

Aims and audience

This book is specifically designed for busy professionals, leaders and decision makers. It is organized in sections that allow you to gain relevant insights quickly and on demand. Above all, the content is grounded in *real-world experience* and practical applications within the context of digital transformation, ensuring its relevance to everyone who has embarked on their digital journey. Each topic concludes with *thought-provoking questions and actionable steps* to guide your personal exploration of AI and its implications.

Ultimately, the book empowers you to become an active participant in this transformative era. It provides a *handbook* for you to construct your own personal guide to surviving and thriving in the age of AI, fostering self-reflection, critical thinking and engagement with others.

By reflecting on your experiences, asking better questions and engaging with others, you can learn to navigate the AI revolution and position yourself for success.

What to expect from this book

To achieve these ambitious goals, the book takes an open discursive approach, placing a spotlight on the role of AI in the digital world and its implications for business and society. It acts as both an introduction to and a commentary on the challenges facing organizations and individuals as digital transformation continues. It is organized as a collection of observations, recommendations and advice to leaders and managers as they seek guidance on how they can be successful in the use of AI in today's digital economy. But more than that, it is a reflection on my own journey in understanding advances in digital technology and their implications for society. It is a personal perspective on how I learned to survive and thrive in the AI era.

As a result, the book is neither a textbook on AI theory, nor a detailed set of case studies on AI use, nor a playbook on how to 'win' with AI. While it contains elements of all of these, it can best be seen as a collection of insights that will be useful as you try to puzzle out what is behind the current surge of interest in AI, why many people believe that we are on the cusp of a major societal shift, and what that means for those of us who might be struggling to adapt to a new way of thinking, working and living. Hence, above all, this book can be viewed as a handbook to help you create your own guide to navigating the age of AI. It is important that as you read you take time to think about AI in relation to your own personal journey over the past few years, your current context, and the future aspiration you hold for yourself and your organization.

- Reflect on your experiences in light of the current AI opportunities and challenges we face.

- Learn to ask better questions about AI's disruptive impact and future directions.

- Find your own voice to capture your perspectives and insights into AI and its use.

- Share your observations about AI with colleagues.

- Connect and engage with others to build relationships, broaden your horizons, and grow the AI-focused conversations that matter to you.

Introduction

Every day it seems that more advanced AI capabilities are announced, an upgraded AI model is released, or an unexplored application of AI comes into focus. Alongside this avalanche of news is an increasingly polarized debate about AI's impact on society.[1] The 'AI doomers'[2] claim that we are presiding over the beginning of the end, while the 'AI boomers'[3] tell us the future has never looked so bright.

With so much going on, it's a confusing time. We are all struggling to make sense of how such digital advances will affect our lives. Will increasing automation and advancing AI displace large parts of existing ways of working? Do we rush to adopt AI tools or wait to ensure more safeguards are in place?

And yet on one thing we can all agree: it's going to take some time to get to grips with AI and its implications. The latest wave of AI advances is bringing significant changes that require us to ask questions about the ways in which we work today and about the kind of world we want in the future.

But first things first. To make progress we all need to reach a more informed position on many of the key issues. We must take some time to explore the background and critical elements of AI.

The rise of AI

The massive interest in and adoption of digital technologies – including machine learning systems and generative AI tools such as ChatGPT, Gemini, Claude and others – have come hot on the heels of the Covid-19 shock. Over several years, businesses and public services were placed under immense stress as our lives were reshaped to cope with the new requirements and context. Thanks to those experiences, a 'new normal' is emerging, supported by the digital products and services so many of us now rely on every day.

For many of us, a key part of the shift that took place was that, with limits imposed on face-to-face contact, our lives moved online. This meant that services were redesigned to incorporate more digital access and operational activities were modified to support digital forms of remote monitoring and management. As the immediate effects of the Covid pandemic receded, many of these digital consequences have remained. Furthermore, the constant march of technology has led to even more focus on technology adoption, particularly regarding the latest wave of AI-based tools.

However, unlike previous digital-technology adoption efforts that focused on using digital technologies to ensure continuity of existing ways of working, this more recent wave could herald a more transformational set of changes driven by the disruptive nature of AI.

From this perspective, recent AI advances are having a profound effect by challenging core aspects of both organizations and our own roles. From healthcare and medical science through to the provision of education and public services, experiments with the latest AI solutions are highlighting opportunities to redefine everyday activities, priorities and relationships. The capabilities delivered by AI create the potential to make these services more accessible to wider communities; to provide more dynamic or personalized service delivery; and to gain deeper insights to be more responsive to those with different needs, cultures, perspectives and resources.

However, all of these promises can only be met if we face up to the reality that AI brings with it a host of significant challenges. While the broad digital transformation of our society inevitably brings concerns about AI tools being used to replace human creativity, or unbounded content generated by AI replacing many kinds of knowledge workers, deeper issues are also at stake. Security, ethics and privacy concerns come to the fore when AI systems play a key role in deciding critical issues such as who will be allowed (or denied) access to services, automating key decisions in the service delivery process, or collecting significant amounts of data on citizen behaviour or client activity. For many people, the rising capability and adoption of AI is not seen as empowering humanity, but rather it is the basis for 'dehumanizing' it by bringing into question an individual's role and status in a society that is increasingly digital, digitized and digitally transformed.

Improving our understanding of AI is therefore now essential. Politicians, policymakers, business people and citizens are actively engaged in a broad debate about the right short- and longer-term approaches to applying AI technologies, about the pace of AI adoption, and about the governance that is required to ensure AI is being developed and delivered responsibly.

Beyond the fringe

As with many such trends, the hype and inflated expectations that surround AI are creating an environment in which ongoing debates are often more confusing than illuminating. Unfortunately, the juxtaposition of conflicting ideas about the direction of AI frequently creates a substantial amount of heat, but rarely much light. So much so that it is easy to forget what is going on beneath the surface. We all need to find a way to grasp the fundamentals that define the shifts that are underway as AI becomes more widely used.

The goal of this book is to help you to face up to this need. It provides a set of perspectives that form a handbook for surviving and thriving in the age of AI based around five main themes.

- *Understanding the digital context for AI*: the digital transformation context that is driving AI technology investment, development and use.

- *Exploring the background to AI*: the core elements of AI and its disruptive impact.

- *Experiencing AI in practice*: a review of the practical lessons from AI adoption and use.

- *Delivering value from AI*: the core issues and priorities for successfully delivering AI-at-Scale.

- *Looking into the future of AI*: strategies and insights for facing an uncertain AI future.

PART I

UNDERSTANDING THE DIGITAL CONTEXT FOR AI

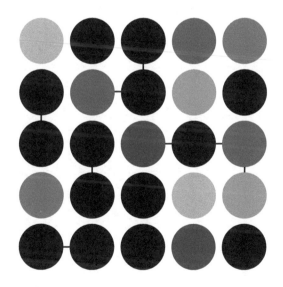

CHAPTER 1

The digital revolution

Is your digital transformation stuck in the slow lane? Explore why a digital revolution demands a radical rethink of your strategy to help you thrive in the new landscape.

With dramatic advances in digital technology arriving every day, many organizations are now focused on how to accelerate their digital strategies to incorporate the latest wave of AI capabilities. From updates to back-office functions to new ways of serving their clients, bringing the power and capability of digital technologies into everyday use is top of the executive agenda.

The ambition may be strong, yet all too often the rhetoric is not supported with sufficiently bold actions. While the specific situations vary, a recurring challenge emerges: executives and leaders at all levels of an organization too often underestimate the scale of the transformation required. They fail to grasp the extent of the digital world's rapid evolution and its disruptive impact on their business. Success requires strong leadership, and the growing sense of urgency must be accompanied by a willingness to redefine core elements of the organization's ways of working.

To achieve this, an important starting point is to accept a new reality: we are in the midst of a digital revolution. From mobile devices and high-speed internet through to AI and quantum computing, we are experiencing rapid, fundamental shifts in digital capabilities across every aspect of business and society. While this declaration of a digital revolution may at first seem unnecessary after several decades of digital-technology adoption, it is important because it serves two crucial purposes.

First, it forces us to question the status quo: if we are living through a digital revolution, what would be the impact of such a profound shift on my organization? How should I rethink our strategy in response to this? Do I have the right skills to be successful in this new era?

Second, by taking this revolutionary stand, the intention is not to sensationalize or exaggerate but to encourage a deeper reflection on the transformative forces shaping the world. Will advances such as AI change relationships between clients and the suppliers of their products and services? Will they reshape organizational structures and decision-making processes? Which organizations will lead this revolution and which ones will fall by the wayside? Recognizing the magnitude of these changes is crucial if organizations are to survive and thrive in the evolving digital landscape.

Talking about a revolution

Accepting the implications of living through a digital revolution offers three key lessons for leading digital transformation.

First, if we admit that we are undergoing a revolution, we are effectively acknowledging that the previous ways in which we looked at the world may no longer be relevant. That is, the applicable models and frames of reference we created to help us understand traditional aspects of our operating environment and predict its future state may no longer be appropriate.[1] In fact, our observations would indicate not only that they are ineffective ways to describe what is happening, but that they may also be dangerously misleading.

For example, think about how your organization describes daily progress across your key projects, or how it defines the learning and development needs of teams to ensure the right skills are available, or how it measures each individual's personal contribution. Are the processes that are in place fit for purpose in a world transformed by digital technologies such as AI? The challenge in a revolution is to try to determine where existing approaches break down, to define more useful perspectives for learning about the elements that matter, and to understand which new ways of looking at the world are going to be more helpful.

Second, the rising tide of digital maturity within organizations increases the tension between those swept along by digital advances and those left behind. This is caused by a widening gap between the cutting-edge digital practices of pioneering teams within an organization and the lagging 'business-as-usual' state of the majority. Where teams experiment with digital-first models, adopting AI tools, they find that traditional structures and management styles must significantly adapt.[2] New organizational forms and operating practices are required to ensure an appropriate mix of innovation with managed accountability.

The simplest approach might seem to be to accept a stark polarization between 'digital-first' and 'digitally supported' factions. However, this simplistic solution creates a harmful side effect. The culture, skills base and physical environment surrounding 'digital-first' teams transforms them into isolated islands of advanced digital experience. Instead of triggering a widespread and rapid adoption of digital practices, this approach backfires, leading to a 'two-speed'[3] organization in which employees experience confusion and complexity. Tensions inevitably arise, and the demand for alternative operational models intensifies.

Third, rather than being able to point to a single cause–effect axis, we are witnessing what commentators such as Eric Brynjolfsson,[4] Andrew MacAfee[5] and Thomas Friedman[6] describe as a confluence of new digital technologies that are pushing us beyond any single advance that we have seen over the last few years. The combination is delivering new insights that would be impossible in isolation, powering innovation across a wide variety of domains, and enabling a recalibration of societal values in determining the balance across the triple bottom line[7] of profit, people and planet.

Furthermore, this digital acceleration shows no sign of slowing down. The pace of change and its significance will only increase as we learn more about how to tie together technology advances in AI, how to use the compute power that is available on-demand, how to broaden deployment of augmented reality (AR) and virtual reality (VR) to provide new world views, and so on.

The recent Covid-driven adoption of digital technologies has highlighted the essential nature of these solutions to our way of life. The 'great acceleration'[8] in digital technology use has been recognized as fundamental to ensure resilience, continuity and adaptability in coping with today's volatility and disruption. The resulting operational practices are both driven by the digital technology and supported by them. Consequently, continuing investment in digital transformation remains a top priority for all organizations.[9]

Why this matters

Highlighting the nature of this digital revolution is not just a point of principle – it has important practical implications. We will never challenge our thinking if we believe that organizational fundamentals remain undisturbed by digital disruption. We will not change the way we work if we see our actions evaluated and rewarded according to outdated values. Whether you are a local authority dealing with adult social care, recycling and potholes or a financial services organization offering payment services, transaction management and insights into people's financial health, the consequences of digital disruption must be addressed. This requires not just digitization of existing operations but significant changes to how we deliver the outcomes now demanded by stakeholders. They are confronted with new ways to interact in rapidly evolving circumstances to meet demands for ever-increasing levels of service quality from their customers.

One of the most challenging aspects of this digital shift is the need to rebalance several levers of business. Assumptions and priorities that have long been in place must now be re-examined. Workers are caught between the need to hold on to their traditions and heritage, while also trying to adjust to new ways of thinking and working.

Consequently, revising ways of working to take advantage of digital technologies such as AI requires organizations to face a series of fundamental paradoxes. Below we highlight five such paradoxes that summarize the profound nature of the challenge to succeed in digital transformation in large established organizations (LEOs) as they seek to survive and thrive in the age of AI.

Paradox 1: be comfortable with being uncomfortable

A primary feature of the digital economy is a lack of clarity about the nature and depth of the disruption faced by individuals, companies and society. All we can assert with any confidence is that the volatility, uncertainty, ambiguity and complexity (VUCA) nature of digital transformation requires organizations to accept this uncertainty and recognize the signals that indicate the onset of substantial changes in their business environment. As a consequence, the traditional values of stability and consistency must be replaced with less certainty in day-to-day operations and new approaches aimed at exploiting future opportunities.

The emphasis, therefore, is on adopting leadership and management approaches optimized for situations of massive uncertainty. Processes and techniques that have been successful in the past may no longer be sufficient. Where they are essential in situations that call for stability and certainty, they may be inadequate when there is a lack of relevant experience, inconclusive data and highly unreliable trends. A move towards greater flexibility based on experimentation is necessary to encourage a culture of continual learning.

Predicting the future is difficult – sufficiently so that some believe the best approach is not to wait but 'to invent the future for yourself'.[10] More than simply being an offhand remark, this statement is in fact an appeal to organizations not to lose hope when thinking about future possibilities. It suggests that all organizations require a bold vision and must engage in actions that will support it. The goal must be to identify meaningful short-term activities that can help the organization test the validity of its vision and how that vision can be delivered.

Paradox 2: keep control by owning less

Many questions are being asked about the appropriate shape and form of organizations fit for a digital economy. At its most simplistic, it has been argued[11] that the advantages of a larger organization's scale and reach are outweighed in a digital economy by the flexibility and speed of change of smaller, more agile organizations.

And yet operational agility is not just a function of size. Questions can also be raised about an organization's assets. Many organizations in the digital economy operate successfully without owning physical assets such as warehouses, trucks, stores or computing infrastructure. Acquiring these capabilities 'as services' to be consumed as and when required can bring operational and fiscal elasticity without a sacrifice of control. If these capabilities are not considered essential to differentiating a company from its competition, then the investment and resources allocated to owning them may be better directed elsewhere.

Such thinking extends to a company's workforce. Organizations can adopt a similarly flexible approach to building skills and capabilities. Many companies, for example, source their critical digital talent from third-party service providers, or use temporary flexible contracts to fulfil needs on an ad hoc basis. The so-called gig economy is one consequence of this thinking.[12]

All of these actions clash with much existing practice, where bigger is often believed to be better. For example, it is difficult to sit around boardroom tables in many organizations and not be confronted with the realization that conventional thinking ensures organizational units are ranked according to size (number of people), spending power (budget allocation) and a leader's seniority based on experience (years of service).

Such thinking is now being questioned. Operating successfully in a digital economy requires an organization to continually acquire new skills to assemble a viable ecosystem, to curate third-party services that meet its needs, and to manage individual performance based on current contribution. The future of organizations may well be smaller core teams but with the support of much wider networks of associates and partners working together through a variety of means, coordinated dynamically around opportunities as they arise, and encouraged with novel, mutually beneficial incentive mechanisms.

Paradox 3: strengthen the organization through exposing weaknesses

Governing a complex organization requires that it is broken up into manageable pieces, each with substantial autonomy and purpose. Typically, the siloed nature of many organizations is a response to a natural, explicit decision to cluster tasks with common aims, and to ensure that teams have local control over all aspects of their remit. Locally made decisions are optimized for the constrained environment in which the team operates. A successful leader defines a clear set of objectives and carves out the resources needed to deliver on time and on budget. Relying on others with different objectives is seen as introducing risk. Successful digital transformation requires bringing together previously siloed groups through improved communication and transparency. To move quickly and with purpose, coordinating cross-disciplinary activity trumps isolated group actions. There are many positive consequences of individuals and teams working together more closely, cooperating more effectively, and synchronizing tasks to avoid duplication and confusion. However, organizations recognize that the transparency provided by this open approach also exposes several shortcomings in their processes, management and operations.

The breaking up of these silos as digital technologies disrupt normal working practices will often shine a light on existing differences in structure, processes and performance. While there is an opportunity here to promote best practices, greater attention is also directed at problematic areas. An organization must have a certain level of resilience to govern wider knowledge sharing and to provide measures to contextualize the information so that it does not distract from the progress being made.

These internal challenges are also seen externally. Digital transformation often involves moves to connect more closely with customers, to engage in co-creative tasks, and to share much more information with partners and other stakeholders. Greater access for stakeholders to the day-to-day activities of the organization with which they interact establishes a relationship of trust. This creates a stronger bond across the organizational ecosystem and increases the organization's core capabilities.

However, many of those in leadership may find this move to greater openness challenging. It can be seen as a threat to an organization's competitive position and an unnecessary step that exposes internal organizational detail best kept under lock and key. Additionally, commercial and regulatory constraints must be factored into any plans. Concerns such as these must be openly discussed, and any resulting issues must be addressed.

Paradox 4: ensure a future by ignoring the plan

A central element of every organization's strategy is the planning process. A great deal of effort and attention is directed towards deciding on future priority actions: prioritizing requests, determining how each of them will be addressed, decomposing them into tasks that must be carried out across the organization, allocating resources, monitoring each task's progress, and performing the interventions necessary to adjust those tasks to ensure successful completion. The focus of many people is therefore to create and manage the plans that act as blueprints for the organization's operation.

Varied in form and detail, these plans are an essential artifact for many organizations. They are often complex, high-profile documents, produced as the centrepiece of elaborate multiyear strategy cycles. They are shared across everyone in the organization, posted on websites and displayed on the boardroom wall. In many situations, questions about the relevance of a given action receive a simple response: it's in the plan.

However, these plans can also become straightjackets restricting an organization's ability to adjust to changing circumstances. Deviation from the plan is considered a failure. Following the plan becomes the objective to be delivered at all costs.

In contrast, digitally disrupted domains must optimize for adapting to unpredictable operating environments. The resulting agile methods have a reputation for increasing flexibility, but often at the cost of adding significant risk into the planning process. Much of the debate around the adoption and scaling of these methods centres on how this flexibility can be maintained while meeting the needs for governance.[13]

Digital transformation initiatives, however, recognize that the unpredictability of the environment in which plans are created deeply influences their value and utility. So much so that in highly volatile situations, some organizations believe that committing to any form of plan is likely to be misleading. How do you plan for a future you are struggling to predict? Addressing this question is the basis for planning approaches that encourage greater experimentation within a rigorous framework that uses direct feedback to define next steps. By using short time-boxed iterations, teams learn quickly and adjust frequently to optimize efforts to the highest-priority needs. Approaches such as 'lean start-up'[14] focus on increasing the speed and depth of learning at the lowest possible cost.

Balancing short-term and long-term success in digital transformation is essential. Neither plans nor the planning process should be abandoned. However, their role and significance should be reviewed. While a plan may have tremendous importance as an operational artifact, in most cases the planning process is just as significant as a cultural and structural ritual that engages and informs everyone in an organization about its relevant priorities and perspectives.

Paradox 5: maintain stability while embracing change

The structures organizations use for governance and decision making have a significant impact. From a cultural perspective, an organization's structure both reflects and determines many aspects of its day-to-day activities. Over the years, complex bureaucratic models have become dominant, where consistency and strong governance throughout the organization dominate.

In contrast, digitally disrupted domains bring significant volatility to an organization's operating context. They introduce new challenges that necessitate organizational structures that balance the need for clear management and decision making with the flexibility required to adapt to varied and evolving contexts. Emerging theories about radical management structures are making it possible to organize business activities around customer-facing opportunities driven by achieving outcomes that optimize customer satisfaction.[15] Similarly, approaches such as 'servant-leadership' are inverting traditional hierarchical styles to democratize key aspects of the management's role in recognizing how important collaboration and teamwork can be when an organization needs to move at speed to deliver successful solutions.[16]

Much of the attention of management scholars is now directed towards these new management styles. Their goal is to define organizational models that balance stable governance with the adaptability required to be successful in a rapidly evolving digital world. Building such flexibility into an organization's infrastructure is essential if it is to maintain relevance in the complex and changing environment we face today.

Live long and prosper

Digital technology advances such as AI are forcing organizations to reassess their current organizational structures and operating models. LEOs faced with adopting digital ways of working must balance the need for substantial change with demands for stability and resilience. In practice, this means they have to address five key paradoxes: being comfortable being uncomfortable; keeping control by owning less; strengthening their organization through exposing weaknesses; ensuring a future by ignoring the plan; and maintaining stability while embracing change. These are big changes, and the struggle to make progress is creating growing tension in many organizations.

Key questions and next steps

How do we rethink organizational models in a digital revolution?

Consider how well the existing organizational models and frames of reference align with the demands of a digital revolution. Traditional approaches to measuring progress, defining learning and development needs, and evaluating individual contributions may no longer be effective in a digitally transformed world. To address this, leaders can initiate a comprehensive review of current practices, seeking to identify where existing approaches break down and exploring alternative perspectives that are more relevant in the context of digital acceleration. This may involve engaging teams in a collaborative effort to redefine key metrics, learning strategies and performance indicators that align with the evolving landscape.

How can digital leaders instil a culture of adaptability and experimentation in organizations accustomed to stability?

Addressing the paradox of being comfortable with discomfort requires a shift in leadership and management approaches. Start by fostering a culture of continuous learning and experimentation. Encourage teams to embrace uncertainty as an opportunity for growth rather than a threat. Implement agile methodologies that prioritize adaptability over rigid processes. Provide training and resources to support employees in acquiring new skills and embracing change. By creating an environment that values agility and experimentation, digital leaders can guide their organizations through the uncertainties of the digital economy.

How can organizations maintain control while embracing a leaner, asset-light operational model in a digital economy where flexibility is crucial?

To address the paradox of keeping control by owning less, reconsider traditional notions of organizational size and asset ownership. Embrace the concept of 'as-a-service' models for non-core capabilities, allowing for operational flexibility without sacrificing control. Explore partnerships and collaborations with external service providers to access resources and expertise on-demand. Rethink workforce strategies by adopting flexible employment models, tapping into the gig economy and leveraging external talent when needed. This shift towards a more agile and scalable operational model allows organizations to stay competitive in the digital landscape without the burden of unnecessary ownership.

How can digital leaders balance the need for transparency and collaboration with the inherent challenges of exposing weaknesses in organizational processes?
The paradox of strengthening the organization through exposing weaknesses requires a careful approach to transparency and collaboration. Aim to promote a culture of openness and learning from failure. Implement communication platforms that facilitate cross-disciplinary collaboration and information sharing. Conduct regular assessments to identify weaknesses in processes and operations, using them as opportunities for improvement rather than sources of blame. Foster resilience within your organization by providing support mechanisms for teams dealing with challenges revealed through increased transparency. By embracing weaknesses as learning opportunities and by reinforcing a collaborative culture, digital leaders can build a stronger and more adaptable organization.

Further reading

Brown, Alan W. 2019. *Delivering Digital Transformation: A Manager's Guide to the Digital Revolution*. De Gruyter.

Greenway, Andrew, Ben Terrett, Mike Bracken and Tom Loosemore. 2021. *Digital Transformation at Scale: Why the Strategy Is Delivery*, 2nd edition. London Publishing Partnership.

Swaminathan, Anand, and Jürgen Meffert. 2017. *Digital @ Scale: The Playbook You Need to Transform Your Company*. Wiley.

CHAPTER 2

A disciplined change approach to digital transformation

Many organizations are rapidly experimenting with AI capabilities and digital tools but struggle to broaden impact from these activities and make required changes permanent. Success depends on overcoming challenges of digital transformation and learning how to avoid being distracted by short-term fixes to build a culture of innovation for long-term digital advantage.

Digital transformation provides the backdrop and context for the AI adoption activities taking place today. But what does digital transformation entail? Rather than simply digitizing existing manual processes and practices, organizations undergo digital transformation when they seek to adopt digital technologies to redesign the products and services they offer, to gain new insights into markets and operations, and to evolve their ways of working to be optimized for the new digital era. As a result, business activities are increasingly centred on digital assets, and their surrounding processes evolve to take advantage of their particular circumstances and opportunities in a digitally disrupted environment. While sectors such as entertainment and online retail were among the first to embrace these changes, the effects of digital transformation are being felt across all industries and sectors.

Yet, managing this digital disruption and propagating the lessons from digital-technology adoption is far from straightforward. No matter how clear and obvious the need for change, attempts to guide an organization across the various barriers to new technology adoption requires skill, persistence and a robust strategy.

Observing how organizations adjust in times of crisis can be very instructive when exploring ways to accelerate digital transformation. Forced into fundamental changes due to the Covid pandemic, it was interesting to see how quickly organizations were able to bring new digital technology onboard and become accustomed to new working patterns. Whether it was hybrid workplace schedules or increased collaboration online, at both an individual and an organizational level operational practices and the supporting infrastructure shifted in record time to adapt to new regulations, disrupted business conditions and changing lifestyles. On a personal level, our daily habits adjusted to allow us to interact in new ways, and a revised set of priorities guided how we spent our time.

It is curious, then, that these experiences are in stark contrast to the challenges organizations traditionally face when introducing sustained changes to their ways of working to take advantage of digital technology such as AI. Surveys and reviews of barriers to digital transformation[1] have highlighted how resistance to change is a major hurdle. In many situations, despite their aspirations to adopt digital technologies and adjust working practices to deliver greater value, organizations struggle to go from early 'quick wins' to more substantial sustained improvement. How can we make sense of these contradictions? And what lessons do they highlight for the current waves of AI adoption?

The digital change paradox

While curious at first glance, there are several ways to understand this change-resistance paradox.

The first obvious comment to make is that unprecedented events such as the Covid pandemic often result in an extraordinary shockwave that affects ongoing practices and forces new ways of thinking and working. These situations help to confirm a well-known principle that substantial change is often driven by one key factor: a compelling reason to act. The recent pandemic and its subsequent impacts were undoubtedly a huge forcing function for change. A response was essential. In well-accepted change models such as John Kotter's '8-Step Process for Leading Change',[2] a clear focus for any change activity is the initial step to create a sense of urgency.

The question, then, is whether organizations view digital disruption as a 'compelling reason to act'. It is certainly the case that many organizations understand this more today than they ever have before. Events such as the Covid pandemic have forced a different perspective on the need to use the digital solutions that are already in place, to embrace additional digital-technology deployment, and to transform operating approaches to be not just digitally enabled but digital first. The use of digital technology was widely heralded[3] as a cornerstone of responses to the instability that the pandemic caused and a substantial element of post-pandemic recovery.

Support for digital-technology adoption was an essential part of every organization's reaction to the pandemic. Comments about the acceleration of digital-technology adoption[4] by Satcha Nadella and other industry experts have stressed the importance of digital ways of working to support remote access to information, group collaboration, device monitoring, online commerce and a great deal more. Without these digital capabilities, our ability to keep functioning would have been severely reduced. For example, a study from the European Intelligence

Unit[5] found a strong correlation between digital maturity and an organization's ability to weather the unprecedented disruption caused by the pandemic.

A second observation concerns the technology-driven nature of many digital transformation initiatives. Experience indicates that managing change across an organization is critical for the success of its digital transformation. However, lessons from the agile software delivery domain have taught us that placing too much focus on the technology can be detrimental.[6] Organizations frequently become overly obsessed with the new capabilities presented by digital technology and get carried away by the excitement of its use by a few experts in high-performing teams. These early results are often deceptive.

Too often we find that digital transformation programmes overemphasize technology acquisition and underemphasize the support required for broad adoption of new practices. To achieve sustained success, organizations need to have a disciplined approach to change, supported by innovation management practices that yield results and grounded in techniques that address the most common failure points. Without an appropriate balance between speed and discipline, engaging in such change can produce chaotic results.

Third, when we consider the latest waves of digital technology, such as AI, we may well be in an early 'honeymoon period', where the initial impact of digital-technology deployment is obscuring potential longer-term issues. Excitement about early pilot deployment is understandable. However, providing digital support across the organization to aid business operations requires a great deal of effort.

What we saw with the Covid situation is illustrative of the issues. The immediate concerns that faced organizations adjusting to the impact of the pandemic forced them into expensive and disruptive emergency initiatives. These were largely successful in meeting organizations' current needs, but they took a heavy toll.[7] In addition to the financial implications, there have been notable negative impacts on the stability and security of technology infrastructure, growing work backlogs and increased levels of individual employee stress.

In fact, in the Covid case, the near-term emergency actions that were essential to maintain business continuity may have derailed in-flight digital transformation efforts. For example, a recent National Audit Office (NAO) review[8] into IT spending in the UK's HM Revenue and Customs concluded that its ten-year modernization plans were delayed due to the need to deal with shorter-term digital delivery obligations. One area highlighted by the NAO is the growing technical debt[9] faced by HM Revenue and Customs because of the slowed-down updates to its aging systems. Pressure on IT teams has meant that previous plans to reduce this risk have had to be shelved.

The concern, clearly, is that short-term experiments with new digital technologies may prove to be a distraction from ongoing systemic improvements to digital infrastructure and operating practices. Excitement about new AI advances may therefore be more disruptive to longer-term digital transformation needs than it is beneficial.[10]

A scalable and sustained approach to digital change

Success in digital transformation requires striking the right balance between seizing opportunities in the short term and applying discipline in managed change to align with the characteristics of the organization and its culture over the longer term. This balance is difficult to establish and even harder to maintain. The experiences from many projects have highlighted that defining and executing a balanced digital transformation strategy is neither straightforward nor without risk.

To mitigate this, as we are seeing with AI adoption,[11] many organizations take their first limited steps on this journey by adopting digital technologies for interacting with customers, by engaging in pilot projects built with commercial or open technology stacks, and by updating parts of their back office with lighter-weight technology infrastructure consumed as a service. Such digitization efforts have yielded useful results, but only when potential disruption has been minimized through appropriate management.

The lessons from experiences with organizations undergoing the trauma of digital transformation highlight the fact that successful, scalable and sustained digital change processes adopt disciplined approaches in three areas.

- They encourage an innovation-focused mindset with support systems and mechanisms for accelerating the path from idea creation to action.

- They actively explore digital business model alternatives to experiment with new ways to create value, drive down costs, build partnerships and respond to client-driven opportunities.

- They assist the organization and its people to become more adept at change by creating a culture where people feel motivated, engaged and supported when trying something new.

These areas of focus bring to the organization the agility and flexibility necessary to embrace digital transformation. Additionally, they surround the deployment of digital technology with the management structures and discipline that are essential to their successful use.

The pathway to digital transformation

To understand the elements of digital transformation in more detail, consider the path towards it as several distinct steps. Based around five main activities, these form a simple framework for contextualizing AI adoption efforts.

This framework for digital transformation defines five necessary areas of focus for understanding the impact of digital technologies. In any digital transformation programme, an organization may be engaged in activities that address one or more of these areas. Organizations frequently proceed in a linear fashion, applying increasing resources and energy as they move through the five elements below, but a much more complex profile of activities is often simultaneously being carried out across these five elements.

Digitization: converting data, transactions and business artifacts into more accessible digital formats

Acquiring and reformatting data to be more accessible to digital processing is fundamental to any digital transformation. Whether this is acquiring new data, converting paper forms to digital records, or converting existing digital data into more usable formats, this step can offer new value-creating opportunities in existing markets and open up new digitally focused markets that were not previously possible. For example, the simple process of moving paper-based forms online does more for an organization than reducing the cost of maintaining physical artifacts. The act of digitizing the paper forms presents new opportunities for how data is created, stored, curated, analysed, connected, shared, transformed and destroyed.

Many of the early use cases for AI are focused in this area. This includes examples such as automated handwriting recognition, voice-to-text translation and the extraction of data from medical images.

Digital process definition: deploying digital technologies and processes to support key business activities

Digital tools and mechanisms are now replacing many established business controls and operational management capabilities in areas such as human resource management, marketing, points-of-sale, help desks and supply chain management. As a result, business operations may be managed more efficiently and redesigned to optimize key business tasks. Many projects upgrading IT infrastructure are consequently key digital transformations because they enable an organization to process information digitally (e.g. deployment of superfast broadband or rewriting customer-facing applications for use on mobile devices).

In AI adoption, a great deal of value is being provided by redefining digital processes using generative AI solutions in areas such as customer support and supply chain optimization.

Digital value analysis: using digital technologies to generate new sources of value by acquiring new kinds of data about products and materials, information flows and individuals' behaviours

Digital technology applies intelligence to the task of creating products, services and devices, offering new insights into their production, distribution and use. Embedding intelligence in consumer goods, for example, allows them to report back on their current performance, communicate with other devices, and adapt their behaviour to their operating environment. In essence, we can say that any physical device can now be wrapped with a digital capability broadcasting information such as its location, environmental conditions and operating status. That digital footprint provides insights into the device's status in use – information that was previously difficult or impossible to obtain.

These capabilities are at the heart of many of the most prominent AI use cases today. In factories, homes and workplaces, data is being collected and processed by complex algorithms to make a variety of predictions and forecasts.

Digital business model innovation: restructuring and redefining existing markets and environments to encourage new digital business opportunities

Examples in many business sectors have highlighted that when digital products and services replace existing physical goods, or when the physical goods generate a real-time digital footprint, the nature of those markets is opened up to severe disruption by new providers with radically different business models.

In the entertainment sector, for example, the move to digital forms of music and video did more than just replace DVDs: it revolutionized the production and consumption of entertainment services. The increasing capability of AI to analyse consumer data has improved understanding of people's consumption of entertainment products in the home, changed pricing policies for media consumption, altered their delivery formats and styles, encouraged new market entrants, and brought a diverse set of offerings to the market. The business model redefinition that first happened in areas such as entertainment is now seen almost everywhere.

Digital organizational redesign: adjusting key elements of an organization's structure and operating model to be optimized for the digital era

Digital approaches to business have led to revised organizational strategies better suited to digital technologies and business models. This has forced changes to management structures, governance schemes and incentive models to support the new strategies.

Many organizations competing in digitally disrupted markets are re-examining how they should organize their work, their supplier networks and their governance bodies. Existing, mature organizations are openly questioning what it means to be a successful company in a digitally disrupted economy.

Meanwhile, newer companies wanting to take advantage of AI advances operate based on radically new forms of management behaviours and alternative decision-making processes. They embed AI into fundamental aspects of their businesses, including procurement, hiring and staff development, product and project management, auditing and compliance. For instance, an AI-driven business looks not just to hire people with different skillsets, but also to attract them and support talent development through sophisticated AI-based planning and forecasting. It also manages staff in smaller, self-organizing teams, encourages them with impact-driven reward mechanisms, and places them in working environments designed to encourage creativity.

Stepping stones on the digital journey

These five elements provide a useful framework for understanding the targets of digital transformation. However, they do little to help define the path an organization should take to increase its digital capabilities in a sustainable way.

Central to digital transformation is the recognition that it should be viewed as 'embarking on a journey' rather than 'pursuing a destination'.[12] That is, rather than a single well-defined shift to a predetermined way of working, adopting new digital technologies should be seen as a strategic direction in response to emerging needs. Far from flicking a switch, introducing capabilities such as those offered by AI demands constant adjustments to take advantage of the opportunities they bring to optimize the value delivered to all stakeholders.

As with any such journey, significant investment is required to manage the steps along the way. Especially in complex situations with many unknowns, a well-defined strategy that can adapt to the terrain is essential. Starting with a realistic description of the landscape, organizations undergoing substantial AI adoption must establish their current position and intended direction of travel before defining milestones that ensure they make steady progress.

As a result, a disciplined change management approach is the foundation for organizations undergoing digital transformation. It brings a structured improvement scheme that points the way forward and keeps the organization's efforts on track.

All management is change management

Organizations that resist change stagnate and become irrelevant. As a result, change management is a core competency to navigate an ever-evolving environment. It addresses where, when and how to adjust an organization's ways of working appropriately. It can even be argued that all management is change management.[13]

Even so, it is surprising how often in practice organizations position their major change programmes as being detached from 'normal' management responsibilities. While the core of the organization focuses on 'business as usual', change activities are treated as separate processes handed off to innovation groups responsible for taking the organization from one stable state to another.[14] In contrast, in the digital age, where change is constant, a disciplined approach to change management must be considered integral to all tasks, with implications for every one of an organization's activities.

Core to the challenges here is that technology adoption rarely happens in isolation. It is usually a response to some need, deficiency or growth strategy. As organizations adopt digital technologies to improve their operating processes, they look to make more fundamental changes across their business practices to take advantage of the capabilities provided. This dynamic forces organizations to accept that an ability to recognize and manage change is essential.

As a result, how change is managed across an organization is a critical aspect of the success of digital transformation, and this is particularly true when it comes to disruptive technologies such as AI. Furthermore, AI adoption at scale requires careful attention to ensure that the updates in technologies and working practices are meaningful and sustained. What can we learn from traditional approaches to change management in relation to AI adoption? Where do they sometimes fall short when an organization is involved in a substantial digital transformation programme?

When agile is fragile

Experiences from many projects highlight that defining and executing a digital transformation strategy is neither straightforward nor risk free. Success hinges on disciplined management aligned with the organization's unique characteristics and culture. When focused on technology deployments, ongoing digitization efforts have yielded useful results, but they have had limited impact without significant attempts to manage the disruption they create to existing ways of working.

In most cases, experiences with new digital technologies such as AI begin with a series of small experiments or pilot studies. Whether locally driven or formally managed as part of an organization-wide initiative, simplified use cases and activities with limited scope are selected to trial the new technologies to learn about their capabilities. In this way, multiple alternative approaches can quickly be examined, knowledge about their key characteristics can be extracted, and confidence about their applicability can be established.

Despite aspirations to broadly adopt digital technologies and adjust work practices, many organizations struggle to move beyond these initial 'quick wins' to achieve sustained improvement. While they succeed in implementing various optimization strategies, scaling and sustaining change remains elusive. We have seen this challenge before in enterprise software development scenarios.[15] Experience with agile software development teaches us that leaders can become overly fixated on new digital capabilities and can carried away with excitement about innovative practices used by a few high-performing teams. To achieve lasting success, organizations require a disciplined approach to change, supported by effective innovation management practices and grounded in techniques that address common failure points. Speed and flexibility without discipline lead to chaos.

Towards a new approach to change management

Unfortunately, the data from recent reviews indicates that many digital transformation programmes are not on track.[16] The fast pace of evolution in the digital world is taking its toll and forcing a review of change management practice. Organizations are having to react more quickly than ever before to the different drivers that challenge the way they define their structure, make decisions and manage the way they operate.

The starting point for accelerating change is to understand your organization's culture. In broad terms, an organization's culture consists of the patterns of behaving, feeling, thinking and believing that pervade the organization's activities and actions. Many studies from eminent management scholars such as Peter Drucker, Gary Hamel and John Kotter have highlighted the importance of cultural awareness in accelerating or dampening change activities. The overwhelming evidence from their work, supported by a variety of practical studies, shows that an organization's culture plays a key role in change activities from two perspectives: alignment with the overall strategy and the extent to which it encourages change. Misalignment in either area creates significant challenges, encouraging individuals to perceive change as increasing operational risk and hindering their motivation to support it.

Accelerating change in an age of AI

For more than thirty years, John Kotter[17] has been a key voice in the world of organizational change, based on his experiences working with many organizations. He has studied the ways in which organizations manage change and adapt to the needs of their clients and stakeholders. The well-known eight-step model[18] that he created in the 1990s offered a very linear view of change as a series of steps that an organization should follow to go from one stable state to another. Derived from existing engineering management practices, the model was aimed at rationalizing chaotic change scenarios in large-scale projects.

Recently, Kotter's perspective has shifted as organizations look to adopt flexible, distributed organizational models more appropriate to a world in constant flux. In this new perspective, organizations must accept that change is a constant and respond with techniques to manage change that is both continuous and emergent.[19] Kotter's latest thinking on how organizations manage change in a digital world emphasizes the need for a move from rigid organizational structures aimed at maintaining stability to more dynamic networks of teams that can respond quickly to an evolving operating environment.

In this new approach, the traditional organizational structures that were designed to 'run the business' in a stable environment must be augmented with a more agile set of teams governed by rapid decision-making processes that encourage creative problem solving. Drawn from all corners of an organization, this dynamic structure creates a responsive layer that plays a dual role: on the one hand, it acts as the first responder to emergent opportunities that can drive growth; while on the other, it insulates the core of the organization from the chaos and instability that often surround these kinds of disruption. This provides a dual operating system that, Kotter believes, is sufficiently adaptable to deal with the volatility that comes with digital transformation.

All change!

All successful digital transformation requires strong leadership. Leaders must champion change, fostering a culture of experimentation and continuous learning. They need to clearly articulate the vision and purpose behind the transformation, ensuring that everyone understands the reasons for the change. Additionally, leaders must empower employees to participate in the change process, providing them with the resources and support necessary to adapt and thrive in the new environment.

In this role leaders are responsible for creating a culture that embraces ongoing change practices. A list of the key facets of this approach follows.

- *Transparency and communication.* Leaders must openly communicate the rationale behind changes and keep employees informed throughout the process. This fosters trust and understanding, making employees more receptive to change.

- *Training and development.* Equipping employees with the skills and knowledge needed to operate effectively in the new environment is crucial. This can involve training people on new technologies and processes, and encouraging new ways of thinking.

- *Empowerment and ownership.* Employees should be encouraged to feel more invested in change. Empowering them to make decisions and contribute their ideas fosters a sense of ownership and increases buy-in.

- *Recognition and rewards.* Recognizing and rewarding employees who embrace change reinforces desired behaviours and encourages others to follow suit. Incentive approaches must be synchronized with the organization's change objectives.

By implementing these strategies, organizations can build a culture that thrives on continuous change. Embracing change management as a core competency, not a separate function, is essential for navigating the ever-evolving digital landscape and the adoption of AI. This integrated approach ensures that digital transformation efforts are not just successful in the short-term but lead to long-lasting, sustainable change that fuels an organization's growth and success.

The latest AI advances continue to drive a rapid shift in the digital landscape, and businesses of all sizes are feeling the impact. While making small adjustments to existing practices is sometimes worthwhile, AI and automation are forcing a more fundamental re-evaluation across industries. From pricing strategies and supply chain management to auditing and compliance processes, organizations are being radically transformed. As a result, digital transformation requires organizations to constantly adapt. Change can be uncomfortable, but delivering it effectively is crucial.

Key questions and next steps

How can we strike the right balance between embracing digital opportunities and applying disciplined change to align with an organization's characteristics and culture?

Begin by conducting a comprehensive organizational assessment to understand the current level of digital maturity, cultural dynamics and existing change management practices. Establish cross-functional teams representing diverse perspectives within the organization to ensure a holistic understanding of both opportunities and challenges. Develop a customized digital transformation strategy that aligns with the organization's culture and values, emphasizing the need for discipline in managing change. Implement regular communication channels to keep all stakeholders informed and engaged throughout the transformation process, fostering a collective commitment to the defined goals.

How can you effectively navigate the complexities of short-term AI pilot studies, ensuring they do not derail broader, in-flight digital transformation efforts?

Conduct a thorough analysis of the AI pilot schemes currently in flight, identifying their impact on ongoing digital transformation initiatives. Expose areas of technical debt and address the negative impacts of AI pilots on technology infrastructure stability and employee well-being. Develop a phased approach to balance immediate operational needs to introduce AI capabilities with the long-term objectives of digital transformation. Collaborate with IT teams to re-evaluate and adjust modernization plans, ensuring that short-term obligations do not hinder the progress of broader digital initiatives. Establish clear communication channels to manage expectations and convey the organization's commitment to sustaining AI in the longer term.

How can you foster a culture of disciplined change that supports innovation, explores digital business model alternatives, and enhances an organization's overall adaptability?

Initiate a cultural transformation by instilling an innovation-focused mindset across the organization. Establish support systems – such as innovation labs and cross-functional task forces – to accelerate the transition from idea creation to actionable initiatives. Encourage teams to actively explore digital business model alternatives through pilot projects and experimentation with different value propositions. Invest in change management training for employees at all levels to enhance their adaptability and resilience. Recognize and celebrate successful instances of disciplined change, creating a positive feedback loop that reinforces the value of embracing change as an integral part of organizational culture.

Further reading

Clayton, Sarah Jensen. 2021. An agile approach to change management. *Harvard Business Review*, 11 January (https://hbr.org/2021/01/an-agile-approach-to-change-management).

Kotter, John P., Vanessa Akhtar and Gaurav Gupta. 2021. *Change: How Organizations Achieve Hard-to-Imagine Results in Uncertain and Volatile Times*. Wiley.

Lee, Jaclyn. 2020. *Accelerating Organizational Culture Change: Innovation through Digital Tools*. Emerald Publishing.

CHAPTER 3

Digital transformation in the age of AI

Understanding the place of AI within digital transformation is vital. AI isn't a magic solution but an extension of existing digital efforts. As organizations embrace AI, they must place their focus on using AI appropriately and responsibly to make sense of data and improve decision making.

Discussions about the potential impact of AI are widespread. Yet, beneath this hype is a real and important need: to make sense of digital advances and find ways to position them in our daily lives. It is a need that has been steadily growing as the capabilities of AI become more widely appreciated.

Over the past decade, broad interest in AI's capabilities was initially sparked by a high-profile gameshow win: when IBM's Watson technology defeated the human competitors on *Jeopardy*, a popular US television programme.[1] Similarly, AlphaGo's comprehensive defeat of an international Go champion created a huge amount of debate about the progress of AI to learn and adapt in new situations.[2] Now, with the arrival of generative AI tools, the conversation has turned to ways in which AI can mimic human skills in ways that allow it to speed up customer service tasks[3] and accelerate productivity in everyday back-office tasks.[4]

The latest wave of generative AI tools has driven the discussion further. While much of the earlier dialogue expressed excitement at the opportunities opened up by AI, we now see concerns being raised with a similar level of passion. One side's focus is on the unlimited potential of such technologies to automate repetitive tasks and enhance creativity,[5] while the other is convinced of the unlimited havoc that this may cause for employment, the economy and society.[6] This clash was highlighted in a widely publicized call for an 'AI pause' to consider the implications of AI adoption and agree on regulations to manage its responsible use.[7]

While the hype surrounding these AI advances has become increasingly intense, the need for a deeper understanding of how AI tools are built and how they operate has never been more urgent. Most importantly, it is essential we go back to basics to be constantly reminded of what lies beneath these tools. Unfortunately, in many cases this fundamental understanding of AI is sadly lacking. The large body of technical materials that now exist may have helped to create a new generation of data scientists and data analysts, but it has done little to help others to gain an appropriate, practical level of insight into the role and impact of AI in business and society.

This is most clearly seen with the availability of generative AI tools. For many people, their high-level understanding of these important capabilities is severely limited. While there are many broad conversations and expressions of concern, it is essential to now focus a great deal more attention on AI to deepen the conversation in two important aspects: what it is and what it can do.

In relation to the first of these questions, there have been several attempts to describe the operational elements of generative AI. This involves describing how the large language models (LLMs) on which they are based are trained by using vast amounts of data to understand and generate natural language and other forms of content. It also addresses the improvements in software and hardware performance that explain why generative AI tools have suddenly exploded onto the scene. Such descriptions vary depending on their source, from high-level overviews in business magazines[8] and broad news channels[9] to detailed reviews[10] and domain-specific analyses[11] from academic research teams.

When it comes to what AI can actually do, we are faced with an endless set of examples of where and how LLMs are being applied to generate outputs for practitioners. A particularly active area is healthcare. Here, we see discussions describing how AI-based solutions may be useful in clinical care and health diagnostics,[12] how they can be used to query large quantities of health data,[13] how they might be harnessed for resolving health care legal disputes,[14] how they could be helpful as the basis for a medical triage service[15] or to improve patient outcomes[16] – and much more.

To gain greater insight into AI we must avoid seeing it in isolation and step back to view it through the lens of the broader digital transformation activities being undertaken in many organizations. Where do such AI advances fit into these ongoing initiatives? How can we situate the latest wave of AI advances in the context of what we have learned about delivering digital transformation?

It's life, Jim, but not as we know it

The current era of AI-driven digital transformation is powered by a convergence of advances in data analysis, access to new digital sources of data, high-speed connectivity, and raw computing power. Seen together, they are enabling rapid advances in how digital solutions are designed and delivered.

The excitement surrounding these digital solutions is justified. After several decades of research and investment, advances in data analysis, data access, connectivity and computing power have finally come together. This powerful combination is accelerating the design and delivery of digital solutions, impacting everything from government services to commercial businesses solutions. The interesting opportunity here is to view this combination of capabilities as providing what we might describe as 'intelligence'.

While stricter and more robust definitions exist, most people now see these broad capabilities as the core of AI. Generally, AI refers to any system capable of mimicking tasks traditionally requiring human intelligence. It is the convergence of these underlying technical infrastructure components that allows us to achieve this. By applying these advances, AI systems can be developed that rely on machine learning: a technique that utilizes vast amounts of data and computing power to build and validate decision-making logic. This logic forms the core of an AI model. The AI system then adjusts its algorithms based on the data fed into this model, which generates human-like responses based on the learned patterns.

In one typical scenario, large amounts of data are gathered from a variety of sensors contained in internet-connected devices. This data could come from many sources: domestic devices in the home, environmental sensors on the street, performance metrics in the workplace, or physical monitoring equipment in a factory. By collecting this information, analysis is possible that explores the data to look for patterns. That is, it enables the creation of algorithms that recognize common situations or anomalies and solve problems by learning from earlier experiences to apply that knowledge in unfamiliar contexts.

It is through the skillful application of these core technologies that AI systems excel at many tasks that were previously thought of as being solely the preserve of humans: processing lots of information, analysing a variety of possible future scenarios, recognizing shifts in operating conditions, identifying similarities and differences in complex information, communicating efficiently across large teams, and so on. AI's support in these tasks can bring huge benefits as we adopt more data-driven approaches to decision making and seek greater agility in taking action. It is because of these benefits that AI is no longer seen as purely a technology issue to be addressed by the IT team: it is firmly on the radar of leaders at all levels in the organization. McKinsey's 'state of AI' survey in 2023[17] found that nearly a quarter of C-suite executives personally use generative AI tools, and more than a quarter of companies that are using AI already have generative AI on their board's agenda. Companies with established AI capabilities are leading the charge in exploring generative AI, and those excelling in traditional AI (those McKinsey calls 'AI high performers') are already outpacing others in adopting these new tools.

Navigating the path to AI

However, taking advantage of AI's capabilities is far from straightforward. Leaders today face the challenge of integrating AI capabilities effectively into their organization, realizing its potential while ensuring it complements, not replaces, human skills and capabilities. How can they get the balance right? This requires a clear understanding of where AI can add value and where human expertise remains irreplaceable.

It is therefore essential to be clear about AI's strengths and weaknesses as seen in current products. In broad terms, today's AI tools excel in the following areas.

- *Data analysis and pattern recognition.* AI is capable of analysing vast amounts of data to identify trends and insights that might escape human awareness, informing decision-making processes.

- *Automating routine tasks.* By taking over repetitive tasks, AI frees up valuable human time and resources for more strategic endeavours.

- *Personalized product and service delivery.* AI-powered platforms can deliver tailored solutions and experiences by using existing data to predict future circumstances and needs.

However, AI currently struggles in a number of areas, including the following.

- *Understanding the nuances of human behaviour.* Getting to grips with the complexities of human interaction – including emotions, motivations and cultural differences – is often beyond the capabilities of current AI systems.

- *Creativity and critical thinking.* While AI can generate new ideas based on existing data, it lacks the ability to think truly creatively or to critically analyse complex situations.

- *Ethical decision making.* The ethical implications of AI decision making, particularly in areas where complex judgements are necessary, require careful consideration and human oversight.

To extract economic and social value from the large amounts of information now being gathered and stored in global information hubs, we – individuals, communities and businesses – need to convert this powerful and ever-expanding resource into meaningful input that can help us with everyday decisions rather than confuse and overwhelm our lives. Far beyond the narrow confines of many current AI use cases, these capabilities hold the promise of supporting us in addressing key issues to improve business productivity, empower citizens, enhance sustainable uses of resources, and enable a fairer society for all.

The focus of change

All of this leaves us grappling with an important question: where does this explosion of activity in AI fit in the broader ongoing digital transformation journeys currently being undertaken in organizations? In particular, how should organizations view the AI advances taking place today in relation to their existing digital strategies and plans? Perhaps the most straightforward answer is that it increases the urgency of and the priority given to many of the key elements of digital transformation programmes already underway in many organizations. Greater use of AI brings additional focus on efforts to raise the maturity of organizations. They adopt digital technologies by changing their ways of working to introduce practices that enable new business models, enhance collaboration and drive experimentation. The resulting digital strategies highlight three areas that are essential to digital transformation in the age of AI: opening up, joining up and smartening up.

Opening up

Digital transformation activities focus on creating more effective communication within and across an organization to improve its decision making and speed up activity. Consequently, in many cases the need for greater transparency in planning, forecasting and decision making has forced a great deal of attention to be placed on establishing a reliable base of data and defining robust data management practices for improving the quality of data. This effort is critical to successful AI solutions that rely on the scale, scope and accuracy of the data on which AI tools are trained and operate.

Joining up

The disconnected nature of many organizations is a major barrier to efficient, informed operation. Digital transformation efforts place a key focus on bringing together multidisciplinary teams across an organization to work cooperatively to deliver value. With emerging AI adoption, a flexible approach to integration across an organization is critical. This demands more agile ways of working that adapt to a very dynamic operating environment.

Smartening up

By becoming more aware of the need for advanced digital skills, many organizations have increased their capacity to manage large data sets, have introduced tools to visualize and analyse data more effectively, and have supported managers to become more evidence-based in their decision making. In doing this, organizations form an important basis for a more disciplined approach to AI adoption. The intelligence created as a result of AI adoption relies on effective and efficient approaches by individuals to manage their training, to query them appropriately, and to understand where and how they can be ethically applied.

*

Understanding the basic capabilities of the digital technologies powering AI is important. It is critical if we are to be responsible users of technology and successful leaders guiding an organization's strategy and motivating colleagues around us. It is not that we all need to be experts in the AI technologies themselves. Rather, we need to know enough about their core capabilities to inform what we do and why we do it. To be effective leaders in the age of AI, we cannot abdicate responsibility for obtaining sufficient insight into AI's operating approach to ensure it is used appropriately and effectively.

The digital way

As discussions of AI and its adoption explode, it is hard not to feel overwhelmed by tools such as ChatGPT, Gemini, Claude and others. The breadth of impacts they will have on how we all live and work is substantial. Some view adoption of AI's capabilities as a kind of alchemy: able to change worthless data sets into valuable insights and actions. Others see AI more in term of continued improvements in core digital technologies, requiring hard work and persistence to be successfully applied in the context of large-scale enterprise change activities.

Whatever your position, AI advances form part of the ongoing digital transformation journey that is already being undertaken across many organizations. A deeper understanding of AI is critical to appreciate the significant role it will play along the way. We can build on AI's momentum to continue to open up, join up and smarten up our ways of working.

Key questions and next steps

How can I ensure my organization has an appropriate understanding of the fundamentals of AI in the context of digital transformation?

Conduct a comprehensive awareness campaign within your organization to ensure all stakeholders – from leadership to frontline employees – have a fundamental understanding of AI. Leverage internal communication channels, training sessions and workshops to demystify AI concepts, emphasizing AI's role as a tool within the broader digital transformation landscape. Collaborate with industry experts and thought leaders to provide insights into the operational elements of AI, specifically LLMs, and their impact.

What are appropriate steps to aligning AI advances with ongoing digital transformation initiatives?

Evaluate existing digital transformation programmes to identify synergies with AI advances. Emphasize the importance of data transparency, quality and management practices to support AI solutions effectively. Foster a culture of collaboration and agility to ensure that multidisciplinary teams can adapt to the dynamic nature of AI adoption. Explore flexible integration approaches to connect AI initiatives seamlessly with broader organizational objectives.

What are the key approaches to drive openness, collaboration and skills development across an organization?
Reinforce efforts to create a more open and collaborative organizational culture that aligns with digital transformation goals. Prioritize transparency in planning, decision making and forecasting, focusing on establishing reliable data foundations. Encourage a flexible approach to integration that adapts to the evolving AI landscape. Invest in upskilling employees to enhance their capacity for managing large data sets, visualizing and analysing data effectively, and understanding the ethical application of AI. Recognize the importance of individual skills in managing AI training and querying processes.

Further reading

Lamarre, Eric, Kate Smaje and Rodney Zemmel. 2023. *Rewired: The McKinsey Guide to Outcompeting in the Age of Digital and AI*. Wiley.

Smith, Brad, and Carol Anne Browne. 2021. *Tools and Weapons: The Promise and the Peril of the Digital Age*. Hodder & Stoughton.

Yao, Mariya, and Kate Koidan. 2024. *Applied Artificial Intelligence: A Handbook for Business Leaders*, 2nd edition. TOPBOTS.

PART II

EXPLORING THE BACKGROUND TO AI

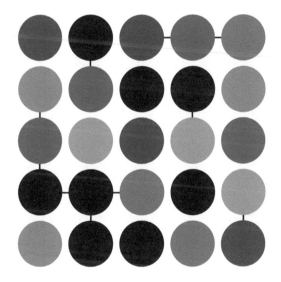

CHAPTER 4

Welcome to the world of AI

AI is transforming our world, from chatbots and movie recommendations to facial recognition systems and self-driving cars. Is AI truly intelligent or is it just sophisticated pattern matching? We can identify seven key ways that AI is being applied that digital leaders should consider.

We live in a confusing world. Technologically speaking, we have entered a period where advances in so-called smart digital products and services are all around us. Often, they are out in the open where they can be seen: your bank's mobile app, for example, or the devices you buy to play music or control the heating at home. However, these capabilities are increasingly buried inside the products and services you have been using for some time: your TV and your washing machine, for instance. A similar thing is happening in the business world.

Much of what we see in today's digital transformation of business involves data-driven innovation bringing predictive insights and automation of tasks we have previously had to do for ourselves. Tedious document checking and reviews have been largely eliminated. Instead of spending hours poring over spreadsheets and PowerPoint slides, it now takes seconds. These advances are changing our relationship with the world around us and challenging our understanding of the the role of human judgement in decision making.

The emergence of AI

At the core of these advances are rapid improvements in digital technology. These days it is hard to escape the rhetoric and promise of what Bill Gates has called 'the new golden age of computer science'.[1] Whether the topic is cloud computing,[2] data science,[3] digital twins[4] or computer architecture,[5] the story seems to be the same: you ain't seen nothing yet! Nowhere is this expectation higher than it is when it comes to AI.

What is AI?

Briefly described, AI encompasses a wide range of technologies and techniques that enable computers to perform tasks that previously required human intelligence. These tasks include visual perception, speech recognition and many forms of decision making.[6] It is considered different from more traditional ways of writing software and solving problems because it operates not through preprogrammed results but by learning from and adapting to data and feedback, so that it can be thought of as evolving independently based on its context, training and learned behaviour.

At its heart, machine learning (ML), a core component of AI, refines problem-solving models and gleans insights from data without explicit reprogramming. It does this using a variety of techniques, such as neural networks[7] and deep learning[8] for modelling data and their relationships.[9] ML can be used to enhance efficiency and competitiveness across various sectors, including finance, healthcare and transportation.

There are numerous ways to outline the core components and attributes of AI and to categorize its diverse characteristics. From a user perspective, one of the most significant distinctions is between two major forms of AI: predictive and generative.

- Predictive AI analyses patterns in historical data to forecast future outcomes or classify upcoming events. It offers actionable insights, aiding in decision making and strategy formulation.

- Conversely, generative AI[10] is designed to create new and original content, such as images, text and other media, by learning from existing data patterns. It enhances creativity and is particularly valuable in creative fields and for innovative problem solving.

All this discussion of looking for patterns in data and making predictions can sound rather mundane. Yet, these AI capabilities, far from being ordinary, are transformative. Andrew Ng, a renowned computer scientist and entrepreneur, likens AI to 'the new electricity',[11] highlighting its potential to revolutionize industries, just as electricity did a century ago. This description emphasizes the versatile power of AI, which makes it an essential tool for all leaders and practitioners to understand and integrate into their ways of working.

The hype surrounding AI is a result of the ease with which these simple concepts can now be applied. The possibilities raised over the past fifty years are now being realized by a convergence of advances in data analysis, access to new digital sources of data, high-speed connectivity and raw computing power.[12] Taken together, they are enabling rapid advances in how digital solutions are designed and delivered. But, more importantly, they are also powering new ways to gather and analyse information, make accurate forecasts, coordinate actions and drive decision making.

The intelligence in AI

The interesting challenge here is to consider how this combination of capabilities can be used to provide what we might view as 'intelligence'. That is, the creation of algorithms that can recognize situations and solve problems by learning from earlier experiences and then apply that knowledge in unfamiliar contexts. Today, achieving that feat mostly relies on using powerful computing resources to sift through massive datasets and explore countless possibilities and variations using knowledge-management techniques.

By 'training' AI systems with a lot of data about known situations, it is possible to use them to compare the new situation with what has been seen before and come to a set of likely conclusions. Then, by feeding back information on the accuracy of its results, the AI system's performance can be tuned over time. Applied broadly, this approach allows AI systems to be used for many things that seem to require 'intelligence', from identifying possible fraud in financial transactions or telling us if it is going to rain tomorrow, through to interpreting medical images or generating the most likely word to appear next in a sentence in response to a query.

So, if the primary techniques currently in use involve high-speed data crunching and statistical modelling, why are people predicting that AI will replace many tasks carried out by humans? Is it really any more than pattern matching based on huge amounts of data that has previously been painstakingly tagged by humans? And does that really amount to 'intelligence'? For many people, these are troubling questions, particularly as AI use becomes more widespread in tasks that are traditionally carried out by leaders and decision makers. To address the concerns, we must delve a little deeper into the role of leadership and look at how leaders approach decision making.

We can understand more about these issues if we consider a common example of AI that is now part of all of our lives: chatbots. These are interactive systems that engage individuals in a conversation to determine their needs and respond with an appropriate answer or a follow-up action. When we look at the 'intelligence' behind the scenes, what we find is quite a simple architecture of data consumption, analysis and response. This has been nicely summarized by Peter Stratton using an example based on how Google's AI chatbot, Duplex, works to help you book a table at a restaurant.[13] He concludes that not only are these systems very narrow in focus (typically aimed at rather constrained actions such as making a reservation, returning a damaged package or finding a required document), they are also heavily dependent on the previous data and interactions they have encountered. Their response is a direct reflection of what they have seen before, with little or no adjustment for individual context, cultural background, sensitivity to environment, and so on.

Furthermore, some experts in digital technology look at AI with a very sceptical eye. Take Kate Crawford, for example.[14] She believes that the combination of massive, curated data stores and extreme computer processing is founded on very dubious ethical and moral thinking. Her analysis highlights why this approach leads to exploitation of data sources, low-wage abuse of workers involved with data tagging, bias in the interpretation of the data due to political pressure, and consolidation of power in the hands of a small number of data hoarders.

Even so, the attraction is that AI-based solutions are beginning to address a very broad set of applications to bring value to a wide set of stakeholders. Kathleen Walch has classified these into seven styles of AI solution that we typically see today.[15]

- *Hyperpersonalization*: using AI to develop individual profiles, and then having each profile evolve and adapt over time based on activities being monitored.

- *Autonomous systems*: applying combinations of hardware and software to accomplish a task, reach a goal, interact with their surroundings and achieve an objective with minimal human involvement.

- *Predictive analytics and decision support*: using AI to understand how past or existing behaviours can help predict future outcomes or help humans make decisions about future outcomes.

- *Conversational AI*: supporting interaction between machines and humans across a variety of media including voice, text and images.

- *Exception management*: applying AI to seek patterns in data sources, learn about connections between data points to match known patterns, and search for anomalies.

- *Recognition*: using AI to identify objects and features in images, video, audio, text or other unstructured data.

- *Goal-driven activity*: learning rules and applying AI to apply those rules to find ways to achieve stated goals in areas such as strategy, role playing and gaming.

Used in isolation or in combination, these patterns of AI use enable us to address many different problem areas. Much of the focus today is on refining the challenges we face to be amenable to these AI patterns.

AI as a prediction machine

The use of AI in making predictions brings new opportunities for many kinds of problem solving. AI acts as a powerful lens for interpreting and harnessing data's potential. Thus, lowering the cost of gathering, managing and maintaining huge amounts of data is critical. In essence, AI is a prediction technology whose results depend on the quantity and quality of the data on which it operates. It excels at recognizing patterns in past data and applying those patterns to anticipate future events. By putting this capability in the hands of everyone, the possibilities appear to be limitless.

Self-driving cars: a paradigm shift in transportation

While describing AI as primarily a 'prediction machine' may sound rather dry and meaningless, consider what it means when we have highly accurate, widely available, low-cost predictive power embedded into everything we do. This predictive capability can now be used to underpin many AI applications, from self-driving cars to personalized medicine. Let us consider the former widely discussed example.

The advent of self-driving cars and other autonomous vehicles epitomizes the transformative power of AI's predictive capabilities.[16] These vehicles are equipped with a suite of sensors to monitor the vehicle and gather data about its surroundings. This real-time data is fed into AI algorithms that analyse the condition of the vehicle and its environment, predict the behaviour of other road users, and make informed decisions about the vehicle's trajectory.

With a constant supply of high-fidelity, accurate data, the core of self-driving car technology is its ability to predict and react to complex driving scenarios. AI algorithms can detect and track objects, anticipate potential collisions, and determine the safest course of action. This predictive power enables autonomous vehicles to navigate roads with remarkable precision and safety, often surpassing the capabilities of human drivers.[17]

In this way, the driving experience is transformed. Yet, more importantly, the implications of self-driving cars extend far beyond an individual getting from point A to point B. They hold the potential to revolutionize urban mobility, reducing traffic congestion, improving road safety and expanding transportation options for those with limited mobility. AI-powered self-driving cars can optimize traffic flow, reducing the time spent commuting and improving overall efficiency. Additionally, their ability to react to incidents more quickly and more accurately than human drivers could significantly reduce accidents, saving lives and minimizing property damage.

As a result, in this scenario we can conclude that it is the concept of transportation that is being transformed by AI.[18] Self-driving cars represent a paradigm shift in transportation, demonstrating the transformative power of AI's predictive capabilities. As AI technology continues to advance, self-driving cars are poised to become ubiquitous, shaping the future of mobility and redefining our relationship with transportation.

And transportation is only one example of how seeing the challenges we face through the eyes of a prediction engine can redefine the world around us. Similar examples can be drawn from domains as diverse as healthcare, education, finance, entertainment and logistics.

When AI technology and economics collide

It is important to note that this dramatic shift of perspective is only possible because we have substantially changed both the technology *and* the economics of prediction. Advances in digital technology have brought together the confluence of faster processors, vast data stores and reliable communications infrastructure with more intelligent algorithms for analysing data. At the same time, more efficient hardware manufacturing processes and a focus on bringing all this technical capability online via easy-to-use tools through cloud-based platforms have redefined cost models to increase access. Through this combination of technical and economic advances, problem solving has been converted from reasonable guesses about what will happen next into robust predictions on which we can rely.

These are not new ideas. They were first described in detail by Ajay Agrawal, Joshua Gans and Avi Goldfarb in their 2018 book *Prediction Machines: The Simple Economics of Artificial Intelligence*.[19] In that seminal book the authors argued that understanding this fundamental concept unlocks the true potential of AI. By recognizing AI as a prediction engine, they believe we can effectively anticipate its impact on the economy and rethink AI's effects on society's future direction.

Their perspective is based on a very simple definition:

Prediction is the process of filling in missing information. Prediction takes information you have, often called 'data', and uses it to generate information you don't have.

Central to their argument is the idea that AI's primary function is not to replicate human intelligence, but rather to create predictions based on existing input. AI algorithms are fed vast amounts of data, allowing them to recognize patterns and generate probable outcomes. By recognizing this shift in understanding, we move beyond the hype surrounding AI and identify its concrete applications in various domains.

One illustrative example from *Prediction Machines* is in the field of medicine. Traditionally, diagnosis relied heavily on a doctor's experience and knowledge. However, AI-powered prediction engines can analyse massive sets of medical data – including images, lab results and medical records – to predict the probability of a certain diagnosis or the effectiveness of a specific treatment plan. Not only does this improve accuracy, but it also speeds up the diagnosis process, reducing suffering, reducing costs and potentially saving lives.

The power of prediction

These important observations from Agrawal, Gans and Goldfarb have huge implications. AI predictions could revolutionize business strategies in many domains. By analysing customer behaviour and market trends, AI is able to anticipate future demand and assist in developing targeted marketing campaigns, optimizing supply chains and proactively addressing potential issues.

As we have seen, AI's predictive capabilities are being harnessed across a wide range of industries, transforming forecasting processes and driving innovation.[20] A few examples of how AI is being used in forecasting follow below.

- *Demand forecasting.* E-commerce companies rely on sophisticated AI models to forecast product demand.[21] These models analyse historical sales data, customer behaviour, seasonality and external factors to accurately predict future demand. This allows businesses to optimize inventory levels, minimize stock disruptions and reduce excess inventory costs, leading to improved customer satisfaction and operational efficiency.

- *Energy consumption prediction.* Utility companies employ AI to forecast energy consumption patterns.[22] AI models consider historical consumption data, weather conditions and economic indicators to predict future energy demand. This helps utilities optimize resource allocation, reduce power outages and plan for infrastructure investments.

- *Financial market forecasting.* AI algorithms are being used to analyse vast amounts of financial data, including stock prices, trading volumes and economic indicators, to predict future market trends and identify potential investment opportunities.[23] AI-powered financial forecasting is becoming increasingly sophisticated and influential in investment decisions.

- *Weather forecasting.* Meteorological agencies use AI to analyse complex weather data – including satellite imagery, radar observations and atmospheric models – to predict weather patterns and generate accurate forecasts.[24] AI algorithms can identify subtle patterns and correlations in weather data that traditional forecasting methods may miss, leading to more precise predictions.

- *Healthcare risk prediction.* AI is being used in healthcare to analyse patient data – including medical history, lab results and lifestyle factors – to predict the likelihood of developing certain diseases or experiencing adverse health events.[25] This information can be used for preventive care, personalized treatment plans and resource allocation in healthcare systems.

These examples demonstrate a few of the diverse applications of AI in forecasting, highlighting its ability to extract insights from large datasets and provide valuable predictions that inform decision making across industries. As AI technology continues to evolve, its predictive capabilities used in forecasting are likely to expand, leading to even more innovative and impactful applications.

The current limitations of AI's predictive approach

Recasting AI as a prediction engine helps us to gain a deeper understanding of the role and impact that AI can play in many areas of our lives. However, we must also keep in mind that AI's predictive power is not without limitations. Bias in data collection can lead to flawed predictions, perpetuating existing inequalities.[26] Additionally, overreliance on AI predictions may blind us to unforeseen circumstances and limit our ability to respond to change dynamically.[27]

Therefore, as AI is used in a wider range of predictive scenarios, several key lessons must be considered.

- *Focus on AI as a prediction machine, not a human replacement.* Instead of seeking to create human-like AI, concentrate on leveraging its predictive power for specific tasks.

- *Mind the data.* Ensure your datasets are comprehensive, accurate and unbiased to generate reliable predictions.

- *Human–AI collaboration is key.* AI predictions are best used as a tool to support and enhance human decision making, not as a replacement for it.

By understanding AI as a prediction technology and keeping these lessons in mind, the potential for enhanced data-driven decision making is enhanced while mitigating its inherent risks. This will create a future in which AI functions not as a human replacement, but as a powerful partner in a collaborative human–machine relationship.

AI: a contrarian view

Before we get too carried away extolling the many positive possibilities for AI's predictive and generative capabilities, it is important to recognize that there are alternative ways to interpret AI's current role and impact. Not everyone shares the opinion that AI will be a force for good, sweeping its way through business and society for the benefit of all. Many people have concerns about the way that use of these advanced computing techniques are being described and used.

These concerns are well illustrated in the work of Jaron Lanier through his views on digital-technology adoption and the impact of AI on society.[28] Lanier is a well-known polymath who has played a significant role in the recent history of digital technology. As described in his Wikipedia entry, he is 'an American computer scientist, visual artist, computer philosophy writer, technologist, futurist, and composer of contemporary classical music'. He is perhaps best known for his work in virtual reality, designing applications for headsets and other devices. In recent years he has been leading work in the research team at Microsoft.

Given his breadth of interests and experiences, it is no surprise that Lanier has a strong and thought-provoking perspective on the current digital transformation of business and society. Overall, his views on how we are adapting to these changes can be referred to as a kind of 'dismal optimism'.[29] That is, while he accepts the existence of several doomsday scenarios and recognizes general concerns for human displacement by AI technology, he sees hope for the future if we can marshal our efforts to dampen the worst excesses of big technology companies, authoritarian governments and a host of other bad actors. Unfortunately, though, it seems his confidence in us being able to achieve that goal is not high.[30]

My AI is not your AI

From Lanier's perspective, what we see today, particularly as highlighted in generative AI tools, is not an authentic form of artificial intelligence at all. Rather, he sees it as a clever way to create mash-ups of artifacts created by humans. Lanier describes the function of generative AI tools as a dialogue between humans and machines to pull together existing materials to create a kaleidoscope of predefined views. In that sense, he believes that what we have now is better seen as a form of social collaboration: human prompts guide algorithms to search through and combine artifacts from libraries of curated materials.

To understand this view, it is useful to place today's investments in AI into perspective. As described by Google's chief decision scientist Cassie Kozyrkov[31] and others,[32] we can see the current euphoria around AI as a natural progression from three distinct phases in its history.

Some years ago, the first wave of AI was developed by and for researchers. The discussions and debates taking place at the time were interesting only to a select few, as this was still strictly the purview of mathematicians, statisticians and data scientists. Others tended to find the work obtuse and irrelevant. Consequently, it resulted in many interesting theoretical outcomes but a lack of meaningful commercial success. A long and painful 'AI winter'[33] was the result.

Subsequently, as computer hardware matured and became more affordable, AI became primarily a technology discussion about hardware advances (e.g. increased capacity to perform calculations and novel architectures for parallel processing) and software infrastructure (e.g. cloud-based service provision and streamlined data engineering technology stacks). Using this technology, AI saw greater success, with massive computational power being brought to bear in scenarios such as game playing and simulation. However, much of the conversation was aimed at technical engineers and IT teams sharing techniques to scale support for AI. The Big Tech solutions that emerged were important, even if the wider business benefits of AI were openly questioned.[34]

In contrast, in AI's latest phase, the emphasis has been to make it accessible to end users through open tools with simple interfaces and low barriers to entry. Sophisticated data analysis and enhanced algorithms are widely available. Yet, the appeal of these tools is primarily a result of their clear application and simplified usage model across a range of text- and image-manipulation tasks. More than 100 million users registered with OpenAI in the space of two months, for example, demonstrating the strong demand for easily accessible ways to experiment with this technology.[35] People are clearly excited, and inspiration is being found for experimentation and investment.

Hence, the conclusion from Lanier, Kozyrkov and others is that the current wave of AI is about focusing more on the people who use AI and less on the technologies creating it. In fact, Kozyrkov takes an even stronger line on current AI use.[36] She makes the point that our current wave of AI is not just about making it accessible to users, it is also about recognizing a major shift in user expectations around AI. Moving the focus away from designing user interfaces and towards exposing the technical capabilities of AI – as well as giving easy access to simple AI services for end users – has changed the parameters of success. End users are finding that it is the utility of the answers that AI tools deliver that is critical. Consequently, in practice many people value a response they can readily use over additional time and effort spent verifying the accuracy and provenance of that response – something that, of course, has serious implications.

Data dignity and ownership

While we could look for a technical basis for this shift in expectations, perhaps we should actually look elsewhere. From Lanier's distinct perspective, this latest wave of over-the-top enthusiasm for digital advances is a form of AI fetishism in which an irrational form of technology worship overtakes rationality. Building on this view, he makes his general perspective on AI very clear:[37]

> My attitude is that there is no AI. What is called AI is a mystification, behind which there is the reality of a new kind of social collaboration facilitated by computers. A new way to mash up our writing and art.

While others, such as Kate Crawford, have made similar comments about the lack of intelligence in much of today's AI,[38] Lanier takes the argument beyond a discussion of the mechanics and algorithms of AI to address the mythology behind a misguided vision of 'machines that can think'. In essence, he challenges common attempts to compare acts of human intelligence with actions carried out by so-called artificial intelligence. As he says, it is rather like comparing the way a human runs to driving a car.[39] Of course a car can go faster. But we would not say that the car is a runner, or ever dream of concluding that human running has been made obsolete. Why would we make such a conclusion when we compare the processing that takes place in the technology behind an AI system with the decision making that occurs in a human brain?

As a result, he prefers to describe much of today's automation in terms of data-driven mash-ups, requiring a great deal of care over how data is harvested, managed and reused. The basis for many of these Big Tech solutions is to source data from across the internet, and Lanier has a long track record of being concerned about the way personal data is being reused (and exploited) by AI and other systems for commercial benefit.[40] Lanier's concerns about this approach – which were carefully described in a 2018 article he wrote for *Harvard Business Review*[41] – resulted in a call for greater 'data dignity': an acknowledgement of the need for open data marketplaces where originators and owners of data are fairly recompensed for their involvement. Lanier is an important voice in a wider call-for-action that has been steadily increasing over the past decade.

Historically, broad access to shared data has been essential. The rapid deployment of the internet brought reliance on the World Wide Web and a host of data-driven services, but that success is a double-edged sword. On the one hand, it has been a key enabler of the emerging digital economy. On the other, though, the internet has become a battleground for the management and control of data,[42] and particularly personal data. The exploitation of this data has many dangerous consequences, including what Shoshana Zuboff describes as 'the age of surveillance capitalism'.[43]

Such concerns have led Sir Tim Berners-Lee, the inventor of the World Wide Web, to believe that the Big Tech companies have too much power and control over data and that they have led the internet astray.[44] He is now focused on reinventing the web based on a new paradigm: one expressed by entrepreneur, investor and academic Irene Ng and her team as 'my data belongs to me'.[45] From this perspective, individuals need to take back power from the Big Tech giants by recognizing that data is a currency.[46] The internet can support a new market in data in which each of us can actively participate if we gain greater agency over the data we create.

This view of greater 'data dignity' and a more rational approach to data ownership may seem rather idealistic. Certainly, some believe that ship has already sailed.[47] Regardless, the views of Lanier and others are important because they challenge us to place today's activities into a broader context as we consider the influence of AI.

The road to AI

Recognizing these different perspectives on our journey to today's adoption of AI is essential to maintain a balanced view of how it can be used responsibly. While many aspects of AI are hotly debated, one thing is clear: AI will play an increasingly important and multifaceted role in shaping the future of business and of society more widely. AI's potential lies in its ability to analyse vast amounts of data, leading to advances in several areas.

- *Data-driven decision making.* AI can automate tasks, generate insights and improve forecasting, fundamentally changing how businesses operate.

- *Enhanced problem solving.* AI can identify patterns, exceptions and anomalies within data, leading to more efficient solutions across various industries.

- *Increased automation.* AI-powered systems can handle repetitive tasks with greater accuracy and speed, freeing up human resources for more complex work.

- *Improved human–machine collaboration.* AI can act as a powerful tool to support human decision making and interaction, such as through chatbots and predictive analytics.

In adopting AI, organizations are finding its value across various application styles, including hyperpersonalization, autonomous systems and predictive analytics. These diverse functionalities hold immense promise for addressing a wide range of challenges across industries.

However, it is also important to acknowledge concerns surrounding AI adoption, especially in relation to how AI systems are developed and used in practice.

- *Ethical considerations.* Data collection and usage for AI training raise questions about bias and exploitation.

- *Limited scope of AI intelligence.* Current AI systems excel at pattern recognition but lack true human-like understanding and adaptability.

AI presents a powerful set of tools with the potential to revolutionize various aspects of our lives. Leaders and decision makers must carefully consider how to leverage AI's capabilities while addressing ethical concerns to ensure a responsible and beneficial future.

Key questions and next steps

How can leaders and decision makers discern the ethical considerations and potential biases embedded in AI technologies?

Initiate a comprehensive review of AI implementations within the organization, focusing on the data sources, processing methods and decision outputs. Establish an ethics committee or integrate ethical considerations into existing governance structures to assess AI applications for potential biases and ethical implications. Collaborate with external experts and industry peers to stay abreast of evolving ethical standards in AI development. Implement training programmes to raise awareness among AI developers and users about the ethical challenges associated with AI technologies. Encourage transparency in AI decision-making processes and solicit feedback from diverse stakeholders to ensure a well-rounded evaluation of ethical considerations.

How can organizations enhance the adaptability and context awareness of AI systems?

Foster collaboration between AI developers, data scientists and domain experts to enhance the contextual understanding of AI systems. Implement continuous learning mechanisms that allow AI systems to adapt to individual context, cultural nuances and environmental sensitivities. Invest in research and development to broaden the focus of AI applications, moving beyond constrained actions to address more complex and diverse scenarios. Encourage interdisciplinary collaboration to infuse domain-specific knowledge into AI algorithms, ensuring a more comprehensive and adaptable approach. Regularly assess AI systems for their responsiveness to evolving contexts and implement updates to enhance their adaptability over time.

What are the different styles of AI solutions and how can they bring value to a wide range of stakeholders and address a broad set of applications?

Use an AI framework such as the seven styles proposed by Kathleen Walch to explore the ways in which AI could be used in your organization. Conduct a thorough analysis of organizational needs and challenges to identify areas where different styles of AI solutions can bring substantial value. Implement a flexible AI strategy that incorporates multiple styles, such as hyper-personalization, autonomous systems, predictive analytics, conversational AI, exception management, recognition and goal-driven activity. Establish cross-functional teams with expertise in various AI styles to ensure a holistic and integrated approach to problem solving. Foster a culture of experimentation and innovation, encouraging teams to explore the potential applications of different AI styles in addressing organizational goals. Regularly evaluate the effectiveness of AI solutions across those different styles, making adjustments to align with evolving business requirements and stakeholder expectations.

Further reading

Agrawal, Ajay, Joshua Gans and Avi Goldfarb. 2022. *Prediction Machines: The Simple Economics of Artificial Intelligence.* Harvard Business Review Press.

Crawford, Kate. 2021. *Atlas of AI: Power, Politics, and the Planetary Costs of Artificial Intelligence.* Yale University Press.

Daugherty, Paul R., and H. James Wilson. 2018. *Human + Machines: Reimagining Work in the Age of AI.* Harvard Business Review Press.

Mitchell, Melanie. 2020. *Artificial Intelligence: A Guide for Thinking Humans.* Pelican.

CHAPTER 5

The past, present and future of AI

It is essential to adopt a realistic outlook about AI's impact. While AI has advanced significantly, progress depends on managing overhyped expectations and meeting challenges to deepen our understanding of what AI is and how best it can be applied responsibly.

Talk about AI is now everywhere: from the major news bulletins on TV to the boardrooms of organizations in every city. On the ground, AI is rapidly transforming our world, holding immense potential to revolutionize a wide variety of fields.

However, to fully grasp this potential and navigate the strengths, weaknesses, opportunities and threats that arise, a deeper exploration of AI's context and background is required. Understanding the history of AI research – from its initial bursts of enthusiasm through periods of disillusionment – allows us to identify both past successes and shortcomings. By learning from the missteps, we can create our own perspective on AI and ensure that our use of the technology remains on a responsible and productive path, maximizing its positive impact both for our organizations and, more broadly, for society. This exploration of AI's journey will equip you and your teams to leverage its future capabilities for the greater good, avoiding the pitfalls that have hampered progress in the past.

The long and winding road to AI

Since the earliest days of computer programming, the aim has been to find ways to instruct a computer to process information and perform actions based on the results.[1] The key challenge in achieving this goal has been to convert the human-based understanding of the problem into a workable solution that can be executed by a computer.

With traditional computer programming based on 'procedural languages', you tell a story to the computer about what you want it to do.[2] You carefully lead it by the hand from one step to the next. Data is explicitly described in great detail, and you tell the computer how to bring all the might of its microprocessor to manipulate that data. The problem is that this only succeeds if you are able to anticipate in advance everything you want the computer to do. The requirements must be fully specified. Data structures need to be described down to the last attribute. And all the activities of the computer must be choreographed in a complex arrangement of interactions. It is laborious, complex work, and it requires an engineering mindset – software engineering, in fact.

In contrast, 'declarative approaches' offer a different vision.[3] What if you could describe what you are looking for, define a few rules of the road, and then set the computer off to find its own solution? You could spend your time thinking about the problem domain, leaving the computer to learn enough to track its way to the answer. On route, by trial and error, it uncovers a vast network of relationships, pathways and dependencies. These are recorded in ways that mean that the next time it faces a similar situation, it does not need to start from scratch to work things out. It can use earlier lessons to pick up where it left off.

The excitement of applying this declarative approach is that it finds its own path to solve problems. Each time it fails or succeeds, it adds to its knowledge base and adjusts its way of working.

By trying large numbers of possible combinations of legitimate options, it stumbles its way forward to finding answers that you and I would never dream of. And in so doing it can be said to be exhibiting a new form of intelligence: artificial intelligence.

Whoa Nelly!

For a while during the 1970s and 1980s the excitement surrounding the application of declarative programming techniques was contagious. These systems learn and adapt the more they are used. They can be let loose on problems they have never seen before and find ways to get to an answer. In many ways, this is just the way you and I solve problems by learning as we go.

Unfortunately, in many cases it turned out that all we had done during that time was to move the problem from one place to another. The challenge we had been facing with procedural approaches was the effort required to understand complex requirements in every detail and the coordination it took to manage the realization of an effective solution. This was made more difficult over time as additional effort was needed to maintain its relevance when errors were discovered, or as the operating environment evolved.

In declarative approaches we had a different concern. This way of working only came into its own if we could do two things: unambiguously describe the goals and outcome of the system; and define the rules governing a meaningful solution. A task such as finding the best move in a game such as chess or Go is therefore ideal. Some forms of simulation and prediction also saw great benefits from using these techniques when regular patterns of behaviour could be described and mimicked, or anomalies highlighted for special attention.

But for everything else it fell short. Instead, most computer applications could best be described, taught and realized as large data management and manipulation efforts expressed using familiar techniques borrowed from the manufacturing and construction industry. For this reason, building software during the last few decades has primarily been viewed as a scientific exploration realized through engineering endeavour. Despite the best intentions of some, complex software systems started to be created in 'software factories', or development work was parcelled out via outsourced contracts to the lowest bidder.[4] AI lost its appeal as people saw it as an obscure intellectual activity with narrow practical applications in solving games and puzzles in new and novel ways.

As a result, expectations for the impact and influence of AI had raced too far ahead of the reality of what could be delivered. Unsurprisingly, interest and funding for many AI initiatives began to dry up. The subsequent 'AI winter'[5] saw a great deal of antagonism towards the technology, such that many efforts to improve practices and build new solutions were marginalized, renamed to make them more acceptable to funders, or simply banished to the fringes of the research world.

Old dog, new tricks

Now, skipping forward several decades, we find ourselves in a new era of excitement around AI. The past few years have seen massive growth in the use of the term and widescale application of AI-based techniques across many aspects of business and society. Also – and perhaps more significantly – AI is now big business.[6] Why?

Things have undoubtedly moved on. The capabilities of computer hardware have changed beyond recognition. Relatively inexpensive home computers now measure their storage in terabytes[7] and CPU speed in billions of floating-point instructions per second.[8] High-end graphics processing units (GPUs) provide astounding performance for complex parallel processing of tasks. Programming languages such as Python[9] offer the ease of procedural programming with access to extensive libraries of sophisticated statistical techniques and data analytics capabilities offered by the likes of GitHub[10] and Google's TensorFlow.[11] These are backed by readily available cloud-based execution platforms from the Big Tech providers such as AWS, Google, Microsoft, IBM and others.

This is a major shift to a new digital era delivering many important advances across broad areas of technology, working practices and society. Several of these advances have contributed to producing an environment in which AI is now ready to flourish. Many great articles and books have been written on how our understanding of AI has evolved in recent years,[12] on how businesses are beginning to apply AI,[13] and on the techniques now being used to make AI usable and accessible to many more people.[14] All of these point to why AI is now back in fashion. They outline the reasons why AI is having more practical impact now than it did in the past.

AI redux

Yet, the realities of this latest wave of AI are nowhere near as clean and clearcut as many of us had hoped. With systems of all kinds diffused with greater intelligence and automated decision-making capabilities, a wide variety of concerns have been raised.[15] Recent exchanges about the role of AI in society have taken a distinctly worrying turn.[16] From enabling a surveillance economy to reinforcing social barriers, and from driving a loss of jobs to the de-humanizing of society, people are questioning why, where and how AI should be managed the deployed. While some are calling for a 'pause for reflection',[17] others want to accelerate digital transformation[18] as part of a bigger geopolitical battle that has implications for us all.

As work in the field of AI evolves and the technology's role expands, such discussions will, and must, continue. But as they do, we must face up to a fundamental concern: defining what is AI and what is not.

Many decades ago, computers were roomfuls of vacuum tubes capable of performing no more than a few dozen simple arithmetic operations per second at the behest of lab-coated scientists and engineers. Even then, visionaries such as Alan

Turing foresaw the potential. The so-called Turing test was the embodiment of how he viewed the relationship between human and artificial intelligence.[19] When it was no longer possible to tell whether a response to a question was generated by a human or a computer, he argued, then we could be said to have created artificial intelligence. And for a long time that was sufficient.

However, computing capabilities have moved on. Rather than a roomful of unstable stand-alone components, computers are sufficiently small, reliable and efficient to be embedded and connected within everyday objects all around us. Systems are designed and built using sophisticated algorithms written in programming languages that support a wide variety of programming paradigms suited to solving problems in every kind of domain.

No surprise, then, that for many people the Turing test is little more than an interesting historical reference: one that long ago became irrelevant as a meaningful litmus test for AI.[20] Mathematicians and computer scientists have moved ideas on AI so far forward that they are almost unrecognizable from the earlier days of designing so-called expert systems written in declarative programming languages. A much richer and more complex set of AI approaches has emerged.

Until recently, much of this work to expand AI was out of view for the vast majority of people (and certainly outside their comprehension). For 'the rest of us', a much more intuitive, down-to-earth perspective was being popularized as core computing capabilities became faster, cheaper and more ubiquitous. Intelligence could be simulated through the use of simpler techniques supported by a combination of high-performance computing and clever programming skills. In effect, a much more practically relevant view of AI emerged.

Smarter than the average bear

This was seen most clearly in a wave of 'smart' solutions and services. Over the past few years, many smart products and systems have taken advantage of the speed, power and connectivity of today's computers to perform tasks that appear to demonstrate intelligence. By repeatedly tapping into multiple data sources, accessing the latest information from the systems to which it is connected, and remembering previous behaviour, sophisticated preprogrammed actions can be carried out.

This has significant implications for many common tasks. For example, your internet-connected 'smart TV' is capable of automatically downloading and installing the latest software to manage its programming, to optimize menus based on your viewing history, to turn itself on and off to reduce power consumption, and to adjust audio settings to suit different situations or to align the sound to the type of programme being watched. Many would count this smart programming as intelligence. Furthermore, as it is not being controlled by a human, it surely must be a form of 'artificial intelligence'.

With such smart behaviour having become widely available, many of us now expect that the environments in which we work and live will use similar techniques to adjust to daily patterns. Information is gathered to ensure that actions and reactions are appropriate to the situations that emerge. Below the surface of these smart systems, very few people are aware of the details of how they achieve these outcomes. That is both good and bad.

Please do try this at home

Of course, AI is much more than preprogrammed responses and faster processors. A lot has been happening to enhance a system's ability to learn, reason and create new forms of knowledge that expand human-based ways of solving problems. These sophisticated knowledge-manipulation techniques are increasingly becoming accessible to all, not least through schemes such as generative AI[21] and the large language models[22] that support them. Application of these techniques is heralding a new wave of smart products and services, and adding new capabilities to many of those already in use. While welcomed, this is inevitably adding to the challenge we all face in determining just what we need to know to apply AI effectively.

We want the technologies around us to merge into the background and become part of the fabric of our lives. Intelligent or otherwise, they should blend seamlessly into the way we live. Yet, to a large extent, this increasing familiarity with digital technologies has given us a false sense of security. Questions are now being asked. What information are these technologies collecting? Who owns the data, and who has what rights to use it? How are decisions being made and who governs them? What regulations are appropriate to guide their use? The list goes on.

To understand more about these concerns, choose one of the so-called smart devices that you see around you and ask yourself some questions about how it works. Consider the data that it collects, shares and consumes. Try to assess how it makes its decisions. Then think about the new capabilities that it will offer as it evolves and learns more about your behaviour. Finally, come to your own conclusion about whether you think it is operating appropriately on your behalf, whether it is exhibiting artificial intelligence, and what that means about your view of the digital world. If you are not sure where to start, here is a list of smart products and services to consider:

- your heating thermostat,
- your car's adaptive cruise control,
- your internet-connected toothbrush,
- your bank's credit rating system,
- your dating app's matching algorithm,
- your email client's prioritization and 'suggested response' features, and
- your online shopping platform's recommended purchases button.

The new normal

For many people, considering the behaviour of smart products in this way is disturbing. As digital technologies become more ubiquitous, we must ask new questions about the activities we undertake and adjust our understanding of the world around us in response. A key part of this is to pause, and to consider everyday devices and the intelligence that is now embedded within them. By collecting and analysing data, these devices are using increased processing power and more sophisticated algorithms to learn about our behaviour and adjust their actions to optimize how they work. As these 'smart systems' rapidly evolve with new capabilities, they will force us to question how everyday devices carry out their tasks and shift our perspectives on what we think artificial intelligence is or is not.

Without wishing to repeat all these arguments, several areas are worth highlighting in relation to previous AI experiences.

- The scalability of AI solutions has improved enormously, largely due to much greater access to data. Using a variety of digital technologies, vast amounts of digital data is now generated across a range of devices embedded in people's homes, in their workplaces, in factories, around cities, and elsewhere. We can store, manage and manipulate that data using widely available cloud infrastructure. Furthermore, investments in robust communications solutions mean that it is technically feasible and financially viable to copy, share, combine and move this data around the globe.

- The scope of AI applications has increased. From initial high-profile demonstrations in game playing,[23] the past few years have seen an explosion of new computing techniques, widening the range of solutions that can be applied. Advances in areas such as deep learning[24] and neural networks[25] allow us to redefine problems to make use of the predictive power of AI and solving them by searching many possible solutions in parallel. Extraordinary advances in computer hardware in the past years have made these computationally intense algorithms feasible.

• The skills required to deliver AI applications are much more available than they have ever been before. Driven by increasing demand, a lot of emphasis has been placed on building the pipeline for new AI-trained workers. With the support of significant government funding, retraining schemes for existing workers have accompanied the creation of a new generation of data scientists, computer scientists and others well versed in the fundamentals of AI.

• The societal norms surrounding AI have evolved to be more accepting of technology-driven decision making. Today, most people have become accustomed to the influence and impact of digital technology. A key effect of the digital transformation we have seen in recent years has been a significant shift in attitudes about the role of digital solutions in how we conduct our lives. This has been supported by changes in many areas of government, in legal systems and in every other aspect of societal infrastructure.

Industry leaders such as Jeff Bezos now talk about us living in a 'golden age' for AI.[26] It is so fundamental to today's digital transformation that the capabilities it brings are now integral to the products and services that we use every day.

Avoiding the mistakes of the past

Yet, once again we need to be cautious. In a scene reminiscent of what was experienced with earlier periods of AI development, we now see an ever-expanding set of expectations for AI. It seems that not a day passes without another declaration being made about how our world will be redefined by the boundless effects of this technology.[27] However, while there is much to be excited about, we are seeing some worrying signs.

The first challenge is that it is becoming more difficult to define what is and what is not AI. The phrase is now so over-used that it has lost all meaning. For some people, the answer is to redefine current efforts at AI and confine them to quite a narrow box.[28] In particular, this view rejects the idea that AI is anywhere close to replacing human-based decision making or supporting unsupervised activities in high-risk scenarios. Rather, we need to accept that most of what is now described as AI is based on rather straightforward algorithms that detect patterns in data. Most of the time these systems avoid any attempt to understand the broader context in which data is used, and they perform minimal analysis on the decisions derived from using the data.

Second, the popular press tends to focus on how AI will replace humans by mimicking human intelligence and demonstrating human-like characteristics.[29] What is clear from currently available AI solutions is that we are still a long way from achieving this in any meaningful way. Both conceptually and practically, AI is not ready to assume human tasks that emphasize empathy, ethics and morality. Despite massive investment, it is difficult to imagine how AI can be placed in positions where decision making is ambiguous and filled with nuance.[30] For example, some believe we are still a long way away from significant AI deployment in areas such as autonomous driving.[31]

Third, we are recognizing that the task of designing and deploying AI systems shares many characteristics with traditional software engineering projects. They require managed teams creating complex solutions that will be used, fixed, developed and upgraded over many years. Furthermore, significant issues must be addressed to ensure that these systems not only meet the technical needs of the problem domain, but that they also fit into the volatile and uncertain contexts in which they operate. Expensive failures building and deploying AI systems have therefore already been seen,[32] and a raft of practical techniques must be used to manage AI projects to ensure delivery success.[33]

The long road ahead

In recent years we have come a long way in raising the importance of AI and demonstrating the insights it can bring. The successes we are experiencing are undoubtedly making a great contribution to digital transformation in many business domains. Yet, some of us with long memories remember how previous generations of AI failed to meet expectations and deliver impact in key areas. Reflecting on those experiences will help to ensure that we focus attention on where AI will be able to deliver value today and that we can overcome the barriers to further success in the future.

Recognizing the challenges is an important step in the acceptance of AI. By focusing on how they will be overcome, we will be able to close the gap between the vision for AI and the reality of the systems being delivered today. More than that, we have the opportunity to demonstrate that AI is on the path to maturity and can live up to the high expectations being defined for this new digital era.

Key questions and next steps

How can I define the boundaries of AI amid widespread overuse and abuse of the term?

Initiate a comprehensive review within your organization to clearly define what constitutes AI in the current landscape. Establish more precise criteria and characteristics that distinguish true AI capabilities from routine data pattern recognition. Foster communication and collaboration among industry peers to collectively refine and standardize the definition of AI, ensuring clarity and accuracy in its application. Educate stakeholders – including employees and senior management teams – about the nuanced distinctions between advanced AI and conventional data analytics to mitigate misinterpretations and align expectations.

What are the best ways of acknowledging the current limitations of AI in emulating human qualities?
Develop a realistic understanding of AI's current capabilities and limitations, particularly in mimicking human qualities such as empathy, ethics and morality. Encourage transparency in communication about AI's strengths and weaknesses to manage expectations effectively. Foster interdisciplinary collaborations between AI researchers, ethicists and domain experts to explore ethical considerations and incorporate human-centric values into AI development. Leverage AI where it excels, recognizing that, for now, certain nuanced decision-making scenarios may still require human intervention.

How do I find the most appropriate techniques to ensure that proven software engineering practices are being applied to AI projects?
Recognize that AI projects share characteristics with traditional software engineering endeavours and that they require careful management. Establish well-defined project teams with expertise in AI algorithms, data science and domain-specific knowledge. Implement proven software engineering practices – including iterative development, continuous testing and robust project management methodologies – to enhance the success rate of AI projects. Address challenges related to the volatility and uncertainty of the operating environment by incorporating adaptive strategies and flexible development frameworks. Foster a culture of learning from both successes and failures in AI projects to iteratively improve practices.

Further reading

Kissinger, Henry, Eric Schmidt and Daniel Huttenlocher. 2022. *The Age of AI: Our Human Future.* John Murray.

Russell, Stuart, and Peter Norvig 2021. *Artificial Intelligence: A Modern Approach,* 4th edition. Pearson.

Siegel, Eric. 2024. *The AI Playbook: Mastering the Rare Art of Machine Learning Deployment.* MIT Press.

CHAPTER 6

The importance of generative AI

AI is rapidly advancing beyond expectations. ChatGPT, Gemini, Claude and other generative AI tools can generate human-like responses and perform a variety of knowledge-generating tasks. Seeing these capabilities being rapidly deployed, leaders are now starting to understand generative AI's potential to disrupt industries, and they are also beginning to get to grips with the ethical challenges it raises.

There are many important lessons we can take away from studying the digital transformation journeys being pursued by companies today, but perhaps none is more important than recognizing that progress toward a more digital way of working cannot be defined and measured as a linear path from A to B. Rather, it is a much more torturous expedition into unknown territory in search of solutions that may resemble nothing we have seen before. It is a leap into the dark. How each organization faces this peril gives an important glimpse into their psyche, structure and culture. It offers a view into crucial areas such as risk management, organizational resilience and decision making.

Current AI is neither artificial nor intelligent

This insight is highlighted more than ever when an organization is faced with significant shifts in digital technology. A great example is how it addresses the rising capabilities in AI. Far from its early roots in science fiction, AI has become a dominant factor in the digital transformation strategies of every organization. Where and how an organization introduces AI may well determine if it survives the challenges of the next few years.

Despite the wide array of opportunities afforded by AI, the key for most organizations is a much-reduced and more manageable set of data-manipulation activities.[1] Microsoft's Kate Crawford summarizes this by saying that most AI in use today is 'neither artificial nor intelligent': it is based on large physical computing resources used to apply brute force to rudimentary data-manipulation techniques.[2]

In practice, Crawford observes, AI is operationalized as an application of statistical analysis tools supported by a growing set of machine learning techniques. Primarily, that means mining data to improve how organizations can learn from past experiences, recognize repeating patterns to automate common tasks, and correlate different signals in that data to predict future events. Based on growing access to digitally derived data sources and increased capability in data management, organizations are investing significantly in ways to understand and use the insights they can gain from this.

This narrow perspective on AI is nevertheless very useful. There are wide practical applications of these activities across many aspects of an organization's service delivery, planning, management and operations. Whether it is identifying online sales trends, determining optimal machine settings in the factory, or recommending additional purchases to clients, the use of AI is an essential component of digital strategies.

But wasn't AI promising to deliver a much more significant disruption than this?

The great leap forward

Let us step back for a moment. As long ago as the 1950s, the Turing test was defined by Alan Turing as a major line in the sand for AI. Could we design machines with sufficient intelligence that a human would be unable to tell whether the answer to a submitted question received a response from the machine or a real person? Turing was convinced that day would soon arrive. However, at the time, and for many years, Turing realized that his 'imitation game' was so far from reality as to be absurd. Computers were large collections of electronics that filled the basements of specially air-conditioned buildings. Paper tape and punch cards were used to feed the computers instructions, and then you waited to receive printed results whenever your job was scheduled to be run later that day. Computers were largely seen as calculation engines focused on relatively mundane number crunching and record-keeping tasks.

However, the leaps in the perception of AI and its application since that time have been profound. As recently as the 1990s, the available computing capabilities fell far short of the vision painted by Turing and others several decades earlier. The excitement about machines imitating humans had been lost. Disappointing results led to an inevitable lack of funding and a loss of confidence in the future of AI. Without the speed and power of today's computing infrastructure, AI suffered what some people called an 'AI winter'.[3]

Much has changed since then. There has been a continual hardware and software revolution over many years – a revolution that seems to know no bounds. Digital technology has advanced beyond all recognition. Today's computing infrastructure is unrecognizable from what represented the state-of-the-practice at the end of the twentieth century.

For many people, the first major signal that AI had significantly shifted came from an unusual source: a US gameshow called *Jeopardy*. In 2011 IBM entered its AI technology, codenamed Watson, into the very popular quiz show.[4] When it won by answering a set of random questions correctly, and better than its human competitors, it became worldwide news.[5] People began to take notice that something was happening in AI that was moving it beyond traditional digitization and into a different realm.

This feeling was reinforced with AlphaGo.[6] For years, the application of AI to boardgames such as chess had been used as a way of estimating the technology's progress. The rules of chess are well defined, and large collections of recorded games can be used to teach AI about strategies that lead to success. Consequently, AI programs have been competing effectively against professional chess players for many years.

The game of Go is different. Played on a 19 × 19 grid with black and white stones, the rules are much simpler than chess but there is a much wider set of permutations of different moves and a baffling array of strategies that have been used in the centuries over which the game has been played. Many believed that AI would never be capable of beating the best human players. And then, in 2015, AlphaGo proved them wrong by beating a high-ranking professional Go player for the first time. It went on to defeat a Go world champion and became arguably the strongest Go player in history.

The reason this is significant is not simply that it was capable of defeating any human in a complex game. It is because AlphaGo demonstrated creativity in how it played. Rather than mining large collections of existing moves to decide on which one to play, it used techniques to learn from its playing experiences to create its own path forward. Often these were moves a human would never have used, but they proved to be more effective than conventional human thinking (such as the infamous 'move 37'[7]). That was quite shocking to many observers. Machines that think?

The cat is out of the bag

For many years, progress with the analytical capabilities of predictive AI technology has been impressive. Across several domains we have seen improvements that are raising the bar on how AI can be applied effectively and efficiently.

The announcement of ChatGPT took us one step further: generative AI.[8] On the surface it looked like many other announcements concerning a conversational AI tool – one designed to enable developers to quickly build and deploy conversational AI agents for chatbots, virtual assistants and other interactive applications. However, ChatGPT is important because it demonstrated two things.[9]

First, it makes it clear to a wide audience that we have now moved beyond the Turing test set seventy years ago. Improvements in speech recognition and text-to-speech translation have been ongoing for many years. What ChatGPT did was provide wide access to a simple interface that demonstrates an ability to produce answers that are not only well constructed and believable but also adopt a human tone. *The Guardian* described it as the best system 'for impersonating humans ever released to the public'.[10]

By responding to submitted questions or described scenarios, ChatGPT is a 'generative pretrained transformer' made to realize Turing's 'imitation game'. It produces a solution that is both plausible and well formed by building on its vast knowledge base to create a new set of answers for the user. What seems to astound people is the breadth of its application and the authority of the responses provided.[11] It can understand a wide variety of languages – human and computer programming – and respond with very realistic information.

Second, ChatGPT turns attention away from rote solutions to narrow problem sets with a focus on efficiency and automation towards the promise of a future AI that drives creativity and broadens what is possible. Whether it is a question about business strategy or a request to generate software to implement a required function, ChatGPT can produce a solution that is generated from existing sources and meaningful in the current context. What is more, this level of AI sophistication is now accessible to everyone.

Take the domain of financial services, for example. AI technologies are already widely deployed in areas such as customer service, fraud detection and rates calculations. They are also providing improvements in productivity, quality and service delivery. However, as digital financial services expert Dave Birch points out, the real disruption in financial services will come 'not when banks are using AI, but when customers are'.[12] He sees ChatGPT's breakthrough as being its enabling of individuals and organizations to interact using AI-powered bots acting on our behalf to deal with the boring and the complex activities of our lives. Service delivery is reimagined in a world where bots act on our behalf to support our needs and look after our best interests.

In this way ChatGPT is significant. It places an emphasis on new forms of interaction, changes in authority and responsibility in carrying out tasks, and open access to sophisticated creativity and solution generation. In so doing it changes the AI focus for many people and raises their gaze to future possibilities beyond their current strategy horizon. Such a change of attitude is an essential step forward if AI is to realize its disruptive role in business and society.

Every silver lining comes wrapped in a cloud

But as well as raising hopes about AI's promise, the announcement of ChatGPT has also reminded us that the advent of AI forces organizations and individuals to address new challenges. From both an operational standpoint and an ethical one, ChatGPT makes us confront some of our biggest fears about the digital world that is emerging.

Consider, for example, the implications of a sophisticated AI tool that has no concept of right or wrong. Ask it a question and it responds with an answer that is plausible and believable. However, it might also be incomplete, misleading or simply false. Those already making use of ChatGPT report that its responses are 'dangerously creative'.[13] That is, its creativity knows no bounds. It certainly has limited understanding of whether its answers are true or false.

This can have disturbing results. Cassie Kozyrkov, chief decision scientist at Google, calls ChatGPT 'the ultimate bullshitter'.[14] It provides seemingly correct answers to anything and everything, but with no filter on what it says. It is incapable of determining what is true and what is not. In her view, it is dangerous precisely because it has no interest in ensuring the validity of its responses. Its only goal seems to be to please its audience with an appealing answer.

Furthermore, ChatGPT is widely available at (seemingly) zero cost. This makes it very attractive across many domains. So much so that more than a million users signed up to it in the first five days after its release.[15] Its potential uses appear to be never ending. But they also bring with them some troubling questions.

Imagine the implications of every student being able to write an essay using ChatGPT to generate the text. Of every company that produces software being able to deploy ChatGPT to create its code. Of every social media channel being clogged with responses created by ChatGPT. The list goes on. What will this do to many of our knowledge-based professions? What are the implications for intellectual property and liability in a world where we cannot tell how information has been generated? How will we evaluate the value and validity of AI-generated responses? Will some – or many, or most – of our existing systems be destabilized by the wide availability of AI-generated responses? These and many other questions must now be considered.

It is with this in mind that Paul Kedrosky, an economist and MIT fellow, refers to ChatGPT as 'a virus that has been released into the wild'.[16] He believes that most organizations are completely unprepared for the impact of ChatGPT. He sees its broad release without restrictions as reckless: a Pandora's box has been opened. With the release of ChatGPT we are now beginning to realize just how much there is still to debate about the future of our digital world.

We are the robots

The promise of AI has taken another major step forward with the announcement of ChatGPT. Its human-like responses and wide knowledge base have wowed many people, but its release also has more significant implications for an organization's digital transformation journey: it helps us to imagine a digital future beyond the confines of our current ways of working. Furthermore, it highlights that this future will only be realized if we face up to the challenges that ChatGPT places in our path. Overall, we have been given a stark reminder that AI-driven digital disruption is a double-edged sword.

Key questions and next steps

How can organizations navigate the ethical challenges posed by AI tools such as ChatGPT, ensuring responsible use and mitigating potential risks?

Establish robust governance frameworks for AI adoption, emphasizing ethical considerations, accountability and transparency. Develop clear guidelines on the responsible use of AI, especially in scenarios where ChatGPT's 'dangerously creative' responses may pose risks. Collaborate with industry peers, regulators and experts to contribute to the development of ethical standards in AI, fostering a collective approach to addressing the challenges presented by advanced AI tools.

How should organizations reimagine work, knowledge-based professions and intellectual property in a world where AI, exemplified by tools such as ChatGPT, can handle complex tasks creatively?

Embrace AI as a tool for creativity and efficiency, acknowledging its potential to augment human capabilities. Invest in upskilling and reskilling initiatives to prepare the workforce for collaborative AI–human environments. Engage in dialogues

THE IMPORTANCE OF GENERATIVE AI   93

with academia, policymakers and industry peers to shape new norms and regulations around intellectual property and liability in AI-generated content. Foster an innovative culture that leverages AI to enhance productivity while addressing potential disruptions to existing systems and governance models.

How can organizations prepare for the unprecedented challenges and disruptions that AI might bring?

Proactively assess the potential impact of AI tools on various sectors and professions. Develop contingency plans to address potential misuse and unintended consequences. Advocate for responsible deployment practices, such as incorporating AI literacy programmes for users to discern AI-generated content. Participate in public discourse and regulatory discussions to shape policies that balance innovation with ethical considerations.

How can organizations strategically integrate AI, acknowledging its transformative potential while mitigating risks associated with tools such as ChatGPT?

Align AI integration with organizational strategies, emphasizing the augmentation of human capabilities rather than replacement. Foster a culture of responsible AI use, encouraging employees to critically assess AI-generated outputs. Invest in research and development to contribute to the evolution of AI tools that prioritize accuracy, transparency and responsible decision making. Collaborate with AI developers, researchers and policymakers to influence the trajectory of AI advancements.

Further reading

Harvard Business Review. 2024. *Generative AI: Insights You Need from Harvard Business Review*. Harvard Business Review Press.
Husain, Amir. 2023. *Generative AI for Leaders*. AM Press.
Suleyman, Mustafa. 2023. *The Coming Wave*. Bodley Head.

PART III

ESTABLISHING
AI IN PRACTICE

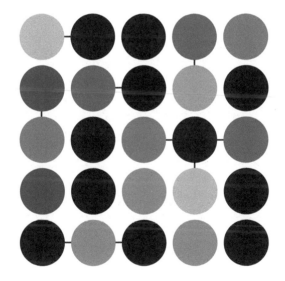

CHAPTER 7

Riding the digital-technology wave

It is essential for digital leaders to stay updated on the latest advances in technology. How can we ride the current AI wave? One approach is to learn how internet adoption took place and relate this to AI's adoption journey.

The past fifty years have seen an astonishing evolution in digital technology. For individuals this has included a range of devices for education, entertainment and personal productivity. In business the changes have been even more profound. Every aspect of the workplace has been affected, from front office to back office, often in quite significant ways. And with the current wave of AI capabilities, the advances seem to just keep coming. Keeping up with these changes is vital. But which ones, and how?

Digital fever

The digital revolution we are now experiencing has changed the face of both business and society.[1] While the pace of progress already seemed unstoppable a few years ago, the past few years have seen even more rapid evolution and innovation in digital technologies.[2] And there are no signs of this relentless pace letting up, either, with new advances constantly revising business operations, reshaping the interaction between the business world and the public, and redefining business-to-business relationships. This has immense implications for business and society alike, and it raises important questions about how organizations and individuals can keep up to date with advances in digital technology, and how they should manage their adoption into current ways of working.

To get to grips with all this, it is essential to place this endless flow of digital technologies into perspective. The power of digital technology to transform our lives is undeniable, and we have all seen first hand the massive potential that digital approaches can bring. Yet, as with any kind of technology, it is easy to focus on the obvious short-term changes to working practices and overlook the deeper longer-term implications. As Roy Amara's law neatly summarizes, 'we tend to overestimate the effect of a technology in the short run and underestimate the effect in the long run'.[3] This observation has proven true time and time again, and digital advances certainly prove the point. Despite the obvious day-to-day changes, organizations of all sizes are still waking up to digital transformation's disruptive impact on their future.[4] In the face of this disruption, they are simply trying to survive.

Staying alive

But standing still is not enough. In today's rapidly evolving business landscape, making use of digital-technology advances is no longer optional: it is imperative for organizations that are aiming to thrive and remain competitive.[5] Embracing and integrating cutting-edge technology into an organization's daily practices can lead to significant improvements across various aspects of business, from enhancing efficiency and productivity to attracting and retaining key staff. There are several important reasons why organizations need to keep up to date with digital-technology advances.

First and foremost, adopting the latest digital technologies enables businesses to streamline their operations and improve overall efficiency.[6] What we have seen is that automation and AI tool adoption can optimize routine tasks, reducing human errors and freeing up valuable time and resources. Together with the implementation of cloud-based services, companies can scale their operations more effectively, minimizing infrastructure costs and improving accessibility for their workforce.

Moreover, keeping up to date with digital-technology advances can significantly boost an organization's competitiveness in the market.[7] Consumers' expectations are continuously changing, and technology plays a pivotal role in meeting those demands. Organizations that integrate digital tools and platforms into their customer service, marketing and sales processes can deliver more personalized and convenient experiences, fostering loyalty and gaining a competitive edge over rivals who are slow to adapt.

Furthermore, attracting and retaining top talent is increasingly dependent on an organization's tech-savviness.[8] In the digital age, skilled professionals seek opportunities to work with forward-thinking companies that invest in their development and provide a dynamic work environment. Employees value flexibility and access to digital tools that enable collaboration and remote work. By staying up to date with digital technology, businesses can demonstrate their commitment to employee well-being and productivity, making them more appealing to job seekers and reducing staff turnover.

Additionally, digital technology can unlock new revenue streams and business models.[9] Companies that create outcome-based approaches and employ data analytics can gain valuable insights into customer behaviour, market trends and operational efficiency, allowing them to make informed decisions and identify untapped opportunities. This data-driven approach can lead to the creation of innovative products and services, opening doors to previously unexplored markets.

Finally, and significantly, staying ahead of technology advances is crucial for ensuring the security and resilience of an organization.[10] The ever-evolving digital landscape brings new cybersecurity threats and challenges. By aligning with the latest technologies and security measures, businesses can better protect their data, systems and reputation.

And still they come

With so much attention focused on the development of digital technologies, it is easy to be overwhelmed by the variety of directions and be overtaken by events as new products come to market. Which ones are essential to drive near-term operational impact? What are their long-term implications for organizational strategy?

A recent set of opinions on these questions come from McKinsey.[11] Released in June 2023, their review of technology trends makes interesting reading for those responsible for guiding their organization's digital transformation journey. Based on a substantial review of data from a variety of sources, McKinsey identifies fifteen technology trends and groups them into five broader categories. Each one is examined by considering the activity undertaken to advance innovation (based on patents and research) and subsequent customer interest (based on news and web searches). These insights are supported by assessments of the investments being made in relevant technologies and their level of adoption by organizations across a wide range of industries. The result is a comprehensive perspective on the technologies that form the core of today's digital transformation portfolios.

McKinsey's review makes several important observations, summarized below.

- *The AI revolution.* Broad application of AI is now seen in almost every domain. McKinsey estimates the potential economic value at stake from applied AI to be between $17 trillion and $26 trillion, and the number of companies pursuing that value has been increasing. Industrialization of machine learning operations (MLOps) is adding to this potential by scaling ML models and greatly reducing the cost of applying ML. By adding the excitement of generative AI solutions to this mix, the AI revolution has now moved into a higher gear.

- *Building the digital future.* Our digital future relies on effective ways to create, deploy and maintain the software that will underpin it. Next-generation technologies are transforming the capabilities of engineers at every stage of the software development life cycle. The software stack is also evolving. Beyond cloud and other communications technology, a particular focus is infrastructure for digital identity management. It is particularly important to bring next-generation solutions to fruition.

- *Computing and connectivity advances.* More effective advanced communications and infrastructure tools are driving interaction and collaboration. They are critical to enabling immersive technology solutions such as virtual and extended reality systems. Additional improvements in the performance of cloud and edge technologies allow even more of these computationally intensive AI solutions to be viable in today's competitive market. Quantum technologies promise yet more computing power and may soon bring completely new ways of solving problems.

- *Cutting-edge engineering.* Several engineering domains are the focus of intense digital innovation. Ongoing advances in autonomous vehicles and aviation, bioengineering and space communication are driving important engineering practices that are being leveraged in other industrial domains. Engineering improvements are being brought to bear on a range of systems, highlighting how digital ways of working can redefine traditional industrial processes at scale.

- *A sustainable world.* As the world becomes more sensitive to the environmental impacts of technology, more attention is focused on renewable energy sources, efficiency of energy use, attempts to reduce carbon emissions, and circular business models. All aspects of digital transformation must now contribute to an organization's sustainability goals in both direct and indirect ways.

Each of these observations is important as organizations move forward with AI adoption. Yet, just as critical is McKinsey's warning about the severity of the digital skills gap being experienced by many organizations as they seek to address these needs. Sourcing digital talent is described as the major barrier being faced today.

Not only do organizations face challenges in finding the right talent, but the McKinsey report foresees 20–30% of the time that workers spend on today's tasks being transformed by automation technologies, leading to significant shifts in the skills required to be successful. Over the coming months and years, the combined disruption from these twin challenges will require a great deal of attention from managers and leaders at all levels of most organizations.[12]

The three phases of the internet

McKinsey's insights into managing technology place an emphasis on the challenges leaders face today as they address continued digital disruption. The latest waves of AI technology will only serve to add to this disruption. How can we ensure that these advances can be leveraged effectively rather than causing additional confusion? Perhaps we can take a lesson from the evolution of the internet: its journey from a complex technology aimed at scientists and researchers into an essential personal aid and business tool in use every day.

Many years ago, when the internet was not yet so embedded in all of our lives, trying to explain it to people was surprisingly difficult. In this first stage of the internet, the use of computers was largely limited to so-called back office tasks: those that took place behind the scenes in areas such as accounting, stock control and complex engineering tasks. Public discussion about the future of computing was primarily a technology debate for engineers and computer scientists, commercialized by a handful of large hardware and software providers. For everyone else it was irrelevant or unfathomable.

By the early 1980s, though, many people who were now involved with the growing wave of software development and the application of computers were becoming excited by the possibilities for wider access to more powerful technology. This was the beginnings of the internet. Its development was aimed at creating a universal infrastructure connecting every computer in the world. By agreeing on the protocols and standards that would support a global platform for integrating applications, everyone would be able to access the digital plumbing required to interact and share information across a vast web of data. Yet, while such sentiments were well meant, their implications for individuals and businesses were unclear. Too few people were able to take advantage of the wide-scale disruptive effects of the emerging internet on business and society.

Then, in the second phase, the value of these standards became clearer as email addresses and webpages started to become more widely popular. Explaining the value of the internet now became so much easier. The era of the World Wide Web had arrived.[13] Here was a use of the internet that gave insight into the possibilities provided by digital technology that everyone could grasp. Rather than focus on the power and possibilities provided by the internal engine of the internet – no matter how extraordinary that was – a simple usage model emerged that made it much more real for many people: they could shop online, connect with friends, apply for government services from home, and so on and so on. Now the challenge had shifted from explaining the intricacies of the technology towards helping people to gain access to these capabilities by getting online. Few understood the mechanisms that lay beneath the surface: the world of internet protocol addresses, universal resource locators, domain name servers, hypertext transfer protocols, etc. The key was understanding enough of the context and capabilities of the internet to be able to assemble its separate components to deliver a robust and repeatable set of actions. At that point in the internet's evolution, that was not easy.

Eventually, of course, all of this work was increasingly simplified and automated in the third phase of the internet. A wide range of tools and services were created to automate much of the work, to check that the details were correct, and to provide user-friendly interfaces to allow ongoing maintenance and updates. For example, in helping people manage webpages, tools such as Wordpress made web hosting much easier, and companies such as Wix, Squarespace and GoDaddy made webpage creation simple and cheap (or free). As a result, access to the internet grew significantly as many more business and individuals used the World Wide Web to advertise, interact and conduct their activities.

The focus was now less on how the internet worked, and more on how to use it appropriately. The most important questions were those focused around the content being created, the audiences being addressed, the best practices for the internet's use, and the ways it could be used to influence information exchange and commerce. We had now progressed to worrying more about the right ways to deploy these solutions, their effects on products and services, and how this new paradigm was redefining lives and livelihoods.

The path to AI

This three-phase journey can also be applied to the path we are now pursuing with AI. While some people have been deeply engaged with its development over many years, for most, the arrival of AI as a meaningful personal, business and societal issue is very recent. It is the more straightforward use cases brought about by tools such as generative AI that have made the difference: these are why AI is seen as more relevant today.

The first phase of AI was dominated by an internal focus on AI technology. It was the domain of engineers and computer scientists looking to understand and improve its performance. Incredible energy was devoted to this work over many years. But for all but a few, this was hidden from view. Beyond news stories about AI winning at gameshows or board games, little was seen of the advances being made.

More recently, the second phase brought with it several more broadly applicable use cases: most significantly, the 'question-and-answer' solutions based on generative AI systems that are now widely available in chatbots and elsewhere. While these represent just a small part of the world of AI, the emergence of ChatGPT, Gemini, Claude and other easily accessible tools has provided a wake up call about how AI-based solutions can readily be applied today by everyone. As millions rushed to play with tools like ChatGPT, the promise of this form of AI hit home in dramatic style.[14]

A key to this popularity has been the straightforward nature of the use cases to which it has been applied: chatbots that query large knowledge bases; text generation to aid a wide variety of writing tasks; real-time language translation; and compelling ways to manipulate text and images. These have quickly captured the imagination of a wide range of individuals and companies. Easy access and simple pricing models have helped encourage a lot of playing and piloting to understand AI's potential. In some cases, the capabilities have begun to be embedded into existing products. Importantly, much of the initial excitement has also fuelled more serious questions about the appropriate use and the challenges of applying AI effectively.

As a result, we have entered the third phase of AI. Increased automation and simplified tools have emerged to reduce the overhead and increase the impact of solutions based on generative AI. Many of them are little more than new interfaces on top of the generative AI engines offered by OpenAI, Microsoft, IBM and others. In other cases, those AI engines have been tuned to support the needs of specific users: lawyers, doctors, educators. With a few clicks, the new tools help people to use these rather complex capabilities to ingest a large dataset, train a large language model, configure an attractive interface for users, or embed these capabilities into the workflow of typical tasks.

Many companies are now releasing products and services that support the application of AI to carry out these different tasks. These are widely available in domains as diverse as sales management, health, education, customer service and legal services. Whether it is small start-up solutions such as ChatNode, for creating data-driven chatbots,[15] or large companies releasing enterprise-ready solutions, such as IBM's watsonx.ai,[16] we are seeing a large number of products and services aimed at simplifying the adoption of generative AI solutions. This is bringing greater access to this technology to a wide set of individuals and companies.

The way of the dragon

In a confusing digital world, it is important to step back to reflect on the path we are travelling and to assess current directions. In so doing, we can see that the journey of understanding and adopting AI technology mirrors the phases of development of the internet. Initially confined to tech experts, AI's accessibility has expanded rapidly, and generative AI systems such as ChatGPT have engaged a broader audience in real-world applications.

Now, with simple use cases such as chatbots, text generation and language translation, a new phase is unfolding: a phase marked by increased automation and more user-friendly interfaces. Exciting AI products are being released by many companies – from sectors as diverse as sales, healthcare, education and customer service – simplifying AI adoption and making it accessible to a wider audience. Just as the internet evolved from complexity to widespread use, we are experiencing the wider effects of AI on our ways of working.

Key questions and next steps

How can organizations stay on top of rapid digital-technology advances such as AI and integrate them into their operations to remain competitive?

Develop a strategic roadmap for digital adoption that aligns with organizational goals. Prioritize technologies such as examples of AI that enhance efficiency, streamline operations and address market demands. Embrace automation and AI solutions that optimize routine tasks, minimize errors and free up resources. Leverage cloud-based services for scalable operations and improved accessibility.

In what ways can organizations leverage digital tools to enhance competitiveness and meet evolving consumer expectations?

Integrate digital tools and platforms into customer service, marketing and sales processes to deliver personalized and convenient experiences. Stay abreast of changing consumer expectations and adjust strategies accordingly. Foster a culture of innovation to swiftly adapt to emerging technologies, gaining a competitive edge by offering cutting-edge solutions and experiences.

How can organizations attract and retain top talent in the digital age, where a company's tech-savviness is a crucial factor in attracting employees?

Demonstrate commitment to employee well-being and productivity by providing access to digital tools that enable collaboration and remote work. Invest in upskilling and reskilling programmes to empower the workforce. Create a dynamic work environment that embraces digital innovation, making your organization appealing to tech-savvy professionals seeking opportunities for development and growth.

How can organizations use AI and other digital advances to unlock new revenue streams and innovative business models?

Embrace data analytics and outcome-based approaches to gain insights into customer behaviour, market trends and operational efficiency. Use these insights to inform decision making and identify untapped opportunities. Foster a culture of innovation that encourages employees to explore new ideas and create products and services that cater to evolving market needs.

Further reading

Davenport, Thomas H., and Nitin Mittal. 2023. *All in on AI: How Smart Companies Win Big with Artificial Intelligence.* Harvard Business Review Press.

O'Hara, Keiron, and Wendy Hall. 2021. *Four Internets: Data, Geopolitics, and the Governance of Cyberspace.* Oxford University Press.

CHAPTER 8

Case studies in AI adoption

All sectors are facing a digital revolution. The adoption of AI technology is the latest in a long line of digital disruptions that have been faced. By exploring several of these, we can learn from past experiences how to navigate AI's disruptive force.

A s digital technologies continue to disrupt the business world and society more generally, it is helpful to look at some specific sectors to explore in detail both what effects AI adoption is having on current ways of working and the pressures it is creating for additional future change. Here we examine three areas that offer a spectrum of experiences on which to draw: education, defence and financial services. We go on to reflect on the broader use of AI for personal data analytics by considering the lessons from a review of one of the most high-profile use cases of AI adoption: the Cambridge Analytica scandal.

AI in education

Today's students and educators must now pass a new test. To add to the perennial challenges, the past few years have seen significant advances in digital technology, bringing with them the power to disrupt many areas of education.[1] As with many other aspects of business and society, those participating in the education sector must get to grips with how to adjust to adopt the new capabilities in a responsible way.

Advances in AI, data science and core computing capabilities will change what is taught in schools, colleges and universities; by whom it is taught; and through what means that teaching is given.[2] Intense discussions about whether to accept or reject widely available tools such as ChatGPT are channelling the debate concerning AI's disruptive force.[3] However, like it or loathe it, digital transformation is forcing major reform in all sectors of education.[4] Examining the pressures and tensions emerging in this domain is useful for anyone who is exploring AI adoption in complex environments.

Another digital brick in the wall

With experiences of the Covid pandemic fresh in the mind of educators, students and parents alike, it is worth remembering that digital technology was vital for continued operation in many areas, including education. For many people, in many countries, the pandemic actually had considerable positive effects when it came to digital education.[5] With schools closed and universities out of bounds, ongoing digitization plans and slow-burning digital transformation efforts suddenly became a top priority. More flexible approaches to education had to be found immediately; ways of teaching and examining students needed to be adjusted; and the expansion of remote access to learning became imperative.

Making these adjustments was a struggle, but with enormous effort (and often at very high cost) a great deal was achieved in a very short time. This also brought with it many positive benefits. For some, education became more diverse, inclusive and accessible. But not for all.[6] Some people – particularly those in vulnerable situations or in disadvantaged circumstances – were not served well by the rapid deployment of digital technologies.

They struggled to acquire expensive or inaccessible computing facilities; they did not have access to quiet, safe spaces in which to study; they lacked local support or direct contact with others; and so on. This created a learning deficit that is unlikely to be recovered any time soon,[7] and it has engendered fear of a continued deepening of inequalities from digital education that may be difficult to reverse.[8]

It is in this context that the impact of current and future digital advances on education must be assessed. The massive interest in and adoption of generative AI tools such as ChatGPT, Gemini, Claude and others have come hot on the heels of the Covid shockwave in education. Little wonder that educators, policymakers, parents and students often disagree about the right short- and longer-term approaches to applying these technologies.

Furthermore, digital transformation of education has implications beyond the concerns about using ChatGPT to write student essays or moving lectures online. It is also about rethinking educational needs and processes for the digital age and reshaping the education sector to deliver the support required to do so. To understand this more fully, it is important to consider separately three key dimensions of the digital journey: the business of education, the process of education, and the delivery of education.

The business of education

Digital transformation is bringing significant changes to the business of education, impacting both educational institutions and the broader education sector. In particular, digital technologies are critical in helping to reduce the cost of education delivery while opening up new revenue streams.

In many educational institutions, the obvious starting point for digital transformation programmes is to reduce the operational costs of education delivery. For example, institutions can save on physical infrastructure, facilities and administrative overheads through the adoption of digital tools and platforms. Furthermore, digital marketing and advertising techniques allow educational institutions to target and attract prospective students more effectively. This is seen with social media, email marketing and online advertising, helping institutions reach a wider and more diverse audience.[9]

Consider, for example, AI-powered tutors that personalize learning plans, answer student questions and automate grading. This will free up educators to focus on more impactful one-on-one interactions. This not only improves efficiency but also allows institutions to potentially reduce class sizes and reallocate resources, increasing both the quality and the efficiency of education delivery.

In addition, the rise of online learning and digital course delivery has opened up new revenue streams for educational institutions. They are now able to offer online courses, degree programmes and certifications to a global audience, increasing both their market reach and their potential student base. In this way, educational institutions have diversified their revenue streams beyond traditional tuition and fees. They can now generate income through online course sales, corporate training partnerships, licensing of educational content, and more.

The process of education

Application of digital technology is reshaping how students learn, how educators teach and how educational institutions operate. Perhaps the most noticeable change is the rise of online learning and remote education. Students can access educational content, interact with instructors and complete assignments from anywhere that has an internet connection, providing flexibility in when and where learning takes place. This is assisted by digital tools and data analytics that enable a more personalized learning experience, using algorithms to tailor content and assessments to individual student needs, pace and learning styles.

One of the most important consequences of the move to online education is that digital platforms can widely expand collaboration among students. Online discussion forums, group projects and real-time collaboration tools enable students to work together regardless of their physical location. This also supports the use of digital assessments and quizzes to provide immediate feedback to students, helping them identify areas of strength and weakness. This timely feedback supports continuous improvement.

An illustration of these advances is seen in how AI is personalizing education by creating intelligent tutoring systems that adapt to a student's strengths and weaknesses, providing targeted practice and real-time feedback to accelerate learning and improve outcomes, all while freeing up teachers' time for more complex tasks and one-on-one interaction.

Through these approaches, digital transformation has increased the flexibility of education. Students have more choice over when and how they engage with learning materials, which is particularly valuable for adult learners and those with work or family commitments. Furthermore, digital assistive technologies such as screen readers and speech recognition software assist students with disabilities to engage with a much wider set of materials.

The delivery of education

Perhaps the most disruptive impacts of digital transformation can be found in the delivery of education, with new methods and technologies having enhanced the accessibility, flexibility and effectiveness of learning. In its most basic form, this is clearly seen in the wide adoption of online learning management systems such as Canvas, Moodle and Blackboard.[10] These platforms provide a centralized space for instructors to deliver course materials, assignments, quizzes and communication tools for students. However, they are also core to the ability to deliver education via virtual classrooms, video conferencing and webinars to support blended forms of synchronous and asynchronous learning. These services are now being enhanced with a range of additional AI-powered capabilities.

Additionally, a growing worldwide digital marketplace for educational content has emerged due to broad acceptance of digital delivery at every level of the educational spectrum. One important consequence has been the rise of massive open online courses (MOOCs).[11] MOOCs offer free or low-cost access to high-quality educational content from top institutions and educators. Learners from around the world can enroll in MOOCs to acquire new skills and knowledge. As a result, educational institutions often combine in-person and online instruction in a hybrid or blended learning format. This approach allows for flexibility while maintaining some face-to-face interaction.

Building on these delivery infrastructures, a wide set of new learning technologies is emerging. Perhaps the most promising of these involve the use of augmented reality (AR) and virtual reality (VR). AR and VR technologies are being integrated into education, offering immersive learning experiences in fields such as science, healthcare and engineering. However, there are many more digital technologies – from gamification to digital twins – that are also beginning to make inroads into a range of education scenarios.

Passing the digital test

Alongside these potential benefits, increasing AI adoption in education is also fostering a broader conversation about how, where and when learning takes place. For example, as these technologies mature they raise broad questions about the role of team-based learning, the concept of a campus-based educational experience, and the future of education in the workplace.

These are fundamental concerns that must be addressed as we enter the age of AI.

Furthermore, the potential benefits of digital technology in education are only realized if the barriers to adoption can be overcome. One significant hurdle is the digital divide among students. While some students have access to high-speed internet and modern devices, others may lack such resources, widening the equity gap in education. Bridging this divide requires institutions to invest in infrastructure and support systems to ensure all students can fully participate in digital learning experiences. Additionally, faculty members may face resistance or hesitancy in integrating technology into their teaching methods, due to either lack of training or concerns about the effectiveness of digital tools compared with traditional methods.

Another challenge educational institutions encounter is the rapid pace of technological advances. Educational technology is constantly evolving, making it difficult to keep up with the latest trends and tools. Doing so requires appropriate technology investment alongside additional hiring and ongoing professional development for faculty and staff. Moreover, the ever-changing landscape of digital platforms and software can lead to compatibility issues and interoperability concerns, requiring institutions to invest significant time and resources in selecting, implementing and maintaining appropriate technologies.

Another issue is that educational institutions recognize that the protection of student data and privacy poses a critical challenge in the adoption of digital technologies. With the increasing use of online learning platforms and educational apps, institutions must prioritize data security measures to safeguard sensitive information. Compliance with rapidly evolving regulations adds an additional layer of complexity to data management practices. Balancing the benefits of digital technologies with the need to protect student privacy requires careful planning, robust policies and ongoing monitoring to mitigate risks and ensure compliance with data protection laws.

The sound of the bell

As we experience a new wave of AI technology innovation, the world of education faces unprecedented digital transformation across three key dimensions.

- *The business of education.* Digital transformation has reduced operational costs and expanded revenue streams for educational institutions. Online courses, degree programmes and certifications can now reach a global audience, diversifying income sources beyond traditional tuition fees.

- *The process of education.* Online learning and remote education offer flexibility, enabling students to access content from anywhere. Personalized learning experiences, aided by digital tools and data analytics, cater to individual needs. Collaboration among students, timely feedback and assistive technologies further enhance the learning process.

- *The delivery of education.* Digital platforms like learning management systems facilitate the delivery of education. Virtual classrooms, video conferencing and webinars support both synchronous and asynchronous learning. Emerging technologies like AR and VR offer immersive experiences, while gamification and digital twins are making strides in education.

As the education sector grapples with these transformations, it must strike a balance between harnessing the benefits of AI advances and addressing their inherent challenges to ensure equitable and effective learning opportunities for all.

AI in defence

The defence sector is an area in which the challenges of driving digital transformation across a complex environment are abundantly clear. Over several decades we have seen widescale deployment of digital technologies in many areas of defence, and ongoing military conflicts such as that in Ukraine now highlight how digital technologies are embedded in every aspect of defence.[12] That conflict has even been described as 'a living lab for AI warfare'.[13] As a result, the defence sector offers important lessons about how to approach advanced technology disruption – just as it has in the past.

In defence of defence

Military institutions in countries such as the United States and the United Kingdom are clearly advanced users of digital technologies. Many examples of sophisticated adoption of AI capabilities can be seen across almost all aspects of defence. However, the effects of digital transformation on military strategy, leadership and decision making are not as easy to determine. Different perspectives on digital transformation in this sector are emerging. One of the most interesting comes from a recent report by Nand Mulchandani and Jack Shanahan entitled 'Software-defined warfare: architecting the DOD's transition to the digital age'.[14]

In their report, published by the Centre for Strategic & International Studies, Mulchandani and Shanahan make several important observations about the challenges facing the US Department of Defense (DOD) due to the current wave of advances in digital technology. Their position is that the best way for the DOD 'to stay competitive in a new warfighting environment' is not just to deploy digital technologies as they emerge, in order to digitize established practices, but to redesign strategies, organizational structures and operational tactics in light of newly available digital capabilities. They do not believe that this is happening as quickly or as comprehensively as required.

Effectively, their position is intended as a provocation to Western governments: they need to overcome resistance to change and accelerate digital transformation of the warfighting function, and they must understand that adopting AI is essential to prepare for a future disrupted by digital ways of operating. As adversaries increase their AI investment, with ambitions to excel in the adoption of digital tools and techniques for achieving their goals, this becomes all the more important. In response, they argue, the DOD needs a new approach that will allow it to be far more flexible, to scale on demand and to adapt dynamically to changing conditions.

Importantly, Mulchandani and Shanahan see learning from digital transformation experiences in other domains as being key to how the defence sector can understand the issues and define a way forward. Every other industry, they argue, has moved to a software-defined approach, in which the adoption of software-intensive systems has completely reshaped industrys' ways of thinking and operating. They believe this transition is inevitable across defence too. Accepting and embracing this approach will force the reshaping of fundamental elements of defence strategy.

It is not unusual to read these kinds of comments about the opportunities and challenges of digital transformation in large complex organizations, such as those in the defence sector.[15] Indeed, they are central to documents such as the UK government's 'Digital Strategy for Defence'.[16] However, by explicitly highlighting 'software-defined warfare', two particularly important aspects of digital transformation are being prioritized by Mulchandani and Shanahan.

The first is a request for increased recognition from military and political leaders that software will play such a key role in the future of defence that it demands an entirely new philosophy. They describe this as being central to operating effectively in a digital age:

> Software needs to be at the core of every business and operating model before any business can hope to gain an enduring competitive advantage. The DOD is no different.

Adopting a software-defined approach will bring a number of advantages in how systems are procured, designed, deployed and evolved. As seen in other domains, a 'software-defined everything' attitude will lend itself to more agile ways of working that are not so reliant on large military platform programmes (e.g. new aircraft carriers, submarines, tanks, etc.) that cost huge amounts to produce, take many years to build and consume major resources to manage, maintain and upgrade. Pivoting in this way will force the military establishment to rebalance their perspective on how they invest in hardware and software in defence.

The second is a clearer focus on the way that decision making must change to aggregate new digital data sources, perform analysis to reason about the current environment, and act decisively even in situations of massive uncertainty. This is particularly relevant to AI adoption. All of this must happen in a digital environment requiring speed of action while hostile forces are seeking to disrupt every aspect of the process.

Mulchandani and Shanahan consider optimization of decision making to be at the heart of digital transformation in every organization. Successful digital organizations, they believe, have redefined many core processes but place a particular focus on out-competing their peers in their ability to understand the context in which they're operating, to review the available options and to making things happen.

This focus on decision-making processes is central to military operations. Traditionally, the 'OODA loop' of observe–orient–decide–act provides the operational context for many elements of decision making.[17] In practice, the report argues, OODA-based decision making consists of a confusing and suboptimal combination of manual steps, digitally supported human processes and automated tasks, and these things are becoming even more difficult to align as a diverse collection of AI technologies become available. A new approach is required to combine these different elements with the flexibility required to adapt to the digitally driven changes we will increasingly see over the coming years. This, the authors believe, is what a 'software-defined' perspective can bring to military strategy and decision making.

The kill chain

One of the ways in which Mulchandani and Shanahan distil the issues being faced in decision making is to focus on the 'kill chain'.[18] While this is a rather emotive phrase, it is commonly used in defence to describe the decision-making path from observation to action. In effect, it is something common to all management and leadership activity:

> A multistep process that involves absorbing information, converting that information into knowledge (actionable intelligence), making a decision, acting on a decision, understanding the consequences of that decision, and refining future actions accordingly.

As Mulchandani and Shanahan acknowledge in the report, much of their thinking in this area is heavily influenced by Christian Brose's book *The Kill Chain*, which was first published in 2020.[19] This important and insightful work delves into the challenges and future directions of warfare in the age of advanced technology such as AI. Brose is a former staff director of the US Senate Armed Services Committee and a US Pentagon policy advisor. His book is a comprehensive analysis describing his perspective on how the US military must adapt to the AI era in order to maintain its dominance in the face of emerging threats.

The book's core theme is the kill chain: the sequential stages involved in successfully detecting, tracking and neutralizing an enemy target. Brose emphasizes that digital transformation and AI technologies are most effective when they are integrated, improving each of the kill chain stages to ensure operational success on the modern battlefield.

Brose also delves into some of the challenges faced when making changes in the defence sector, which is the epitome of a large established organization. In particular, based on his personal experiences and observations he outlines the intricacies of military bureaucracy and the barriers to adopting new technologies within the US government. He emphasizes that a more agile and streamlined decision-making process is a necessity for keeping up with the pace of technological developments and therefore countering potential adversaries effectively.

Perhaps the key point of the book is that Brose draws attention to the need for new ways for the military establishment to operate with the emergence of disruptive technologies such as AI, autonomous weapons, cyber capabilities and advanced sensors. He argues that the traditional approach to warfare, which relies heavily on large and expensive platforms such as aircraft carriers and manned fighter jets, is becoming outdated and unsustainable. Instead, he advocates for embracing new, innovative and more cost-effective technologies to stay ahead of adversaries.

Throughout the book Brose highlights the challenges the US faces in maintaining its military supremacy, and he discusses the fundamental shift that is required in the way US military leaders and politicians think about acquisition and use of military technology. He believes that recent events in the South China Sea and in Ukraine provide a wake-up call to policymakers, military leaders and others. There is an urgent need, Brose argues, for transformative change in the defence sector to adapt to operating in a digital world.

A digital future for defence

For leaders and decision makers in every domain, the lessons from the defence sector are all too clear. In a world reshaped by digital technologies of many kinds, it is important to recognize the disruptive nature of the transformation they drive in organizations that are adopting them. In domains such as the defence sector, the pressures created by this disruption can be particularly intense. Internal struggles to redesign and implement digital ways of working must be addressed, while at the same time the operating environment and mission are being redefined due to emerging digital threats. As made clear by the Centre for Strategic & International Studies paper extensively discussed above, this disruptive force is affecting the US DOD markedly, and new attitudes, processes and strategies are emerging as a result. The analysis and recommendations provided are highly relevant for defence, but they also offer important insights for every organization faced with improving their approaches to decision making in uncertain times.

AI in financial services

Even before the latest digital-technology revolution, financial institutions were at the forefront of innovation.[20] From the early adoption of the telegraph for rapid communication to the development of automated teller machines (ATMs) to streamline branch operations, the industry has consistently sought ways to leverage technology for operational efficiency and improved customer service. As a result, a great deal can be learned by exploring approaches to AI adoption in financial services.

Digital technology in financial services

Financial services were among the first sectors to utilize computers and the internet, doing so for online banking, electronic trading platforms and sophisticated data analysis for risk management and investment strategies. This willingness to adapt and to integrate new technologies has transformed how financial services operate and it has opened doors to entirely new products and services, shaping the financial landscape we experience today.

And in recent years, the financial services sector has experienced a further profound transformation: one propelled by AI. A survey from the Economist Intelligence Unit in 2020 underscored this shift, revealing that 77% of bankers believe that AI's capacity to unlock value will be the differentiating factor determining a bank's success or failure.[21]

It is no surprise, then, to observe that AI has already been leveraged in various ways: to augment banking efficiency, bolster security measures and enhance customer service. There are several notable areas of impact.

- *Customer service.* AI-powered chatbots offer round-the-clock support, addressing inquiries, facilitating transactions and furnishing account information. This frees up human representatives to tackle more intricate issues, thereby optimizing resource allocation. Goldman Sachs, for instance, has reported that their implementation of AI-driven chatbots has resulted in significant savings, reduced customer waiting times, minimized call rerouting and decreased hiring needs.[22]

- *Fraud detection.* AI algorithms meticulously scrutinize extensive datasets to pinpoint anomalous patterns or suspicious activities in real time, significantly improving a bank's ability to pre-empt fraudulent transactions. For example, Danske Bank reports that adoption of an enterprise-scale analytic solution harnessing AI has led to a 60% reduction in false positives (with the potential to grow to 80%) and a 50% increase in true positives.[23] This has empowered them to concentrate resources on genuine fraud cases.

- *Loan approvals.* AI can swiftly evaluate a borrower's creditworthiness, speeding up loan approval decisions and refining their accuracy. Balancing this efficiency with use of techniques that address the inherent biases in the loan approval process is pivotal.[24]

- *Personalized banking.* AI scrutinizes customer data to offer tailored product and service recommendations, crafting a more pertinent and engaging banking experience. Numerous banks are broadening their data sources beyond conventional credit scores to tailor financial products, catering to the needs of minority communities.[25] By analysing a wider spectrum of customer data – including rent payments, phone bills and utility payment histories – fintech firms are extending a greater range of financial services to historically marginalized groups than was the case in previous decades.

- *Risk management.* AI aids in evaluating the risk associated with various financial products and services, enabling banks to make well-informed decisions regarding resource allocation. For instance, HSBC's implementation of AI-based mathematical optimization technology has empowered the bank to adjust credit limits based on customer risk, reward and engagement levels.[26]

- *Regulatory compliance.* AI automates tasks such as compliance with Know Your Customer and Anti-Money Laundering, streamlining a bank's ability to meet regulatory requirements. For example, Infosys reports that financial institutions are increasingly deploying AI to surmount challenges associated with existing rules-based approaches, known for their sluggishness, their manual nature and their bureaucratic practices.[27]

The emergence of generative AI

These AI use cases in financial services predominantly take advantage of the predictive capabilities of AI. Boosting existing efforts to adopt AI, the financial sector is witnessing the emergence of a new wave of investment in generative AI. Unlike previous advances, generative AI requires a significant paradigm shift across multiple dimensions if financial institutions are to reap its benefits. A recent McKinsey report highlights several key challenges.[28]

- *Transitioning from task-specific to ecosystem-wide adoption.* Generative AI offers transformative potential extending beyond singular tasks, unlocking a spectrum of advanced analytical capabilities. It requires leadership to grapple with novel concepts such as reinforcement learning and convolutional neural networks.

- *Data as a core node.* While banks have embraced agile methodologies and cloud adoption, generative AI mandates data as a pivotal third pillar requiring close coordination. This entails deeper integration of data and analytics across the entire value chain, fostering enhanced collaboration between business and analytics teams that have traditionally been separated.

- *Unprecedented speed of adoption.* While mobile banking, for instance, took years to surpass online banking, generative AI tools are being integrated rapidly. Examples include Goldman Sachs's adoption of AI for automated test generation[29] and Citigroup's leverage of generative AI to assess new capital regulations.[30] This rapid pace can strain the operating models of less agile institutions.

- *Talent acquisition and training.* Scaling generative AI hinges on an institution's existing talent pool. Leading financial institutions possess a robust foundation in quantitative analysis, modelling and data translation, and this can be leveraged to acquire skills that are specific to generative AI: prompt engineering and data curation, for example. Organizations that lack such expertise must implement costly strategic talent recruitment and training initiatives.

Despite these challenges, generative AI offers substantial benefits to the financial services sector. McKinsey emphasizes several key areas in which it is extending and augmenting more established uses of AI.[31] Most visibly, virtual assistants are being powered by generative AI to streamline customer service, guiding loan officers and providing pre-approved document templates. This frees up human employees to focus on more complex interactions. More broadly, generative AI models act as intelligent assistants, empowering employees by processing vast amounts of data. This includes AI summarizing regulations, generating research reports or creating instruction manuals. All of this translates to valuable time being saved for human employees, who can then focus on strategic tasks.

In terms of customer benefits, generative AI is increasingly being applied to generate personalized content in real time, allowing financial institutions to tailor marketing and sales materials to individual customer profiles. This level of personalization is being used to significantly enhance customer experiences.

Finally, IT operations is another area where generative AI is having a major impact across many sectors. Generative AI is revolutionizing software development, which is a core capability for all major financial institutions. Code-writing AI assistants can translate legacy code and support developers with debugging and testing, ultimately accelerating the software delivery process.

Meeting the high expectations for AI

All of these potential uses and early successes of generative AI are leading to high expectations for its widespread deployment across financial institutions. For example, analysis of the potential adoption of AI across different banking roles undertaken by Accenture indicates that 73% of the time spent by US bank employees has a high potential for being impacted by generative AI: 39% by automation and 34% by augmentation.[32] Furthermore, generative AI's potential reaches into virtually every part of banks and insurance companies, from the C-suite to the front lines of service, and in every part of the value chain. Yet, despite the opportunity and optimism, it is important to be cautious with the pace of AI adoption. Experience with digital-technology adoption over several decades has revealed that optimistic forecasts from technology proponents often face challenges when confronted with the reality of effecting significant shifts in organizations operating within rigid governance structures, relying on aging legacy technology and navigating complex regulatory environments. All these factors must be addressed in defining an appropriate strategy to leverage AI effectively.

An *illustrative* scenario

Based on these opportunities and challenges, formulating an appropriate AI strategy for financial organizations is anything but straightforward. This is aptly illustrated in the hypothetical scenario described by Thomas Davenport and George Westerman in a recent *Harvard Business Review* case study.[33] They highlight the issues by portraying a clash between the ambitions of technology leaders in a financial services organization and the budgeting and governance constraints faced by finance and risk management executives. It is a dramatization of a situation that is commonly being experienced in the board rooms of many financial services institutions today.

In Davenport and Westerman's example, the CEO of a fictional bank contemplates a substantial investment in AI proposed by the head of AI innovation to fund a large-scale plan to transition the organization into an AI-first bank. This proposal entails significant staff restructuring, with AI assuming most customer interactions and human staff concentrating their focus on complex issues and high-value customers.

In contrast with the head of AI innovation, the CFO exhibits caution regarding the proposed move. They express concerns both about losing the human touch – potentially alienating customers and employees – and about the substantial cost and uncertainty of project success, drawing from past experiences with cost overruns in major digital transformation endeavours over the preceding two decades. In this familiar scenario, the CEO is caught between two opposing viewpoints. The potential benefits of AI clash with the importance of maintaining a human connection with customers and a more measured approach to AI adoption. The decision regarding the extent and pace of AI investment will determine whether the bank remains a traditional institution, gradually digitizing to enhance operational efficiency, or undergoes a significant transformation, embracing AI-at-Scale and redefining itself for a new era of financial service offerings.

While this illustration is fictitious, its core characteristics reflect many of the issues currently confronting the financial sector. A recent report from UK Finance and the global management consultancy Oliver Wyman examined AI utilization within financial services, and it too found opportunities and associated risks for the sector.[34] The comprehensive analysis draws insights from a snapshot survey encompassing twenty-three companies, including multinational entities, mid-sized banks and non-banking financial services firms. The findings reveal that a significant majority (70%) of the surveyed firms are currently in the pilot phase for generative AI, with many particularly focusing on 'co-pilot' type tools aimed at enhancing employee efficiency in content production. However, it is anticipated that the realization of returns on investment for more sophisticated applications will typically take between three and five years.

Interestingly, three-quarters of these financial services firms express confidence in the benefits to be derived from generative AI, with the primary advantages foreseen in productivity enhancement and operational streamlining rather than in customer-facing or revenue-oriented contexts. Notably, a trial conducted by the global professional services firm Marsh

McLennan involving a generative AI assistant yielded positive feedback, with 94% of users reporting increased productivity.[35] Alongside this confidence, many important concerns are also highlighted in the survey. The report states that 95% of the surveyed firms are investing in actively factoring AI risks into their control frameworks, and a significant proportion (60%) have already implemented measures to mitigate the risks associated specifically with generative AI.

Lastly, a notable consensus emerges when it comes to the the importance of collaborating with regulators, with four out of five financial services firms agreeing that it is a necessity. Such collaboration is seen as instrumental in promoting best practices in AI deployment and in fostering the development of an internationally aligned regulatory framework.

Challenges and the road ahead

While AI offers a promising future for financial services, there are hurdles to overcome. Just as in other sectors, tackling issues such as cybercrime and ensuring customer data privacy and security within chat interfaces are paramount. Furthermore, training AI models to understand the nuances of financial services language is another challenge. Finally, fostering customer adoption through education and user-centred design is crucial for successful AI integration.

In addition to these common challenges, success in financial services requires particular focus on compliance with regulations. For responsible adoption of AI, a vigilant approach to regulatory compliance is essential. This is highlighted by the Bank of England's investigations into AI, which emphasize the need for a balanced regulatory framework that supports innovation while mitigating potential risks to consumers, firms and financial stability.[36] The Bank concludes that a key step involves clarifying how existing legal requirements apply to AI usage. Additionally, new industry standards and codes of conduct are necessary that instil trust in users by ensuring AI systems adhere to widely accepted ethical norms appropriate to financial services. AI is fundamentally reshaping the financial services sector. From fraud detection and credit risk management to personalized customer service and efficient operations, AI's impact is undeniable. As the industry embraces the latest generative AI, the key will be to balance the need for fast-paced innovation in products and services with the responsible adoption of AI technology in large established organizations. The pressure on digital leaders to get this balance right is intensifying.

AI in personal data analytics

Collecting and analysing personal data on individual behaviour is one of the most high-profile targets for AI use. Whether it is in marketing, human resources (HR), sales or any other aspect of business, learning more about the actions of employees and clients is considered key to efficient and effective performance. However, this does not come without risks. In a world that is increasingly being measured and managed with AI, the fear for many is that the digitally empowered will increasingly exploit AI technology for their own personal gain, manipulate laws in their favour, and influence politics and society through data-driven targeting of individuals and groups. The poster child for many of these fears is the Cambridge Analytica scandal.[37] Much has already been said and written about this, but the results of a three-year investigation provide an opportunity to reflect on the broader lessons of AI analytics adoption.[38]

Ever since the earliest definitions and discussions of the digital economy in the 1990s, concerns have been expressed about the influence that digital technologies might have on our behaviours and the impact they might be able to exert on our society and institutions.[39] These fears were exemplified for many by the Cambridge Analytica scandal concerning the 2016 US election. The company had been using data gathering and analysis to influence elections in many parts of the world over several years. However, with its activities between 2013 and 2016, affecting both the UK's Brexit referendum and the US presidential election, it was accused of obtaining large amounts of data from Facebook without users' consent to target political advertising and influence the results.[40]

After the reports of these activities surfaced in 2018,[41] there was a great deal of discussion about the sophisticated AI technologies employed by Cambridge Analytica, and the way these technologies had been harnessed to change the actions of many people. Was it really the case that election results could be changed by those with the digital knowhow to nudge people's thinking in one direction or another? A report from a detailed government investigation into Cambridge Analytica considered this question.[42]

The report is a great reminder that, in the world of AI and data science, not everything is as it seems. The Cambridge Analytica story illustrates this perfectly. The analysis of large amounts of personal data to learn more about an individual's behaviour was combined with a barrage of prompts to nudge opinions and convert indecision into action. This was no trivial matter of influencing a purchasing decision or getting someone to 'like' a video: the techniques had huge implications when technology, data surveillance and politics collided.

However, as outlined by Laurie Clark's article in the *New Statesman* that summarized the report, the substantial three-year investigation by the UK Information Commissioner's Office concluded that there was no evidence that Cambridge Analytica had misused data to influence Brexit or to aid Russian intervention in elections.[43] What is more, the investigation expressed a great deal of doubt about the claims of Cambridge Analytica in two key areas with important implications for our broader understanding of the role of AI in practice.

The first key finding was that Cambridge Analytica was not doing anything novel in its application of AI and data science to understand and analyse personal data. The investigation found that the data science techniques that the company used were common. There was no magic to what they did to gather data, examine it and make predictions. What they were able to achieve would have been possible for anyone with access to the commonly available technology, the right infrastructure and the requisite skills.

The second critical comment from the review was to cast doubt on whether the approach of data-driven microtargeting by Cambridge Analytica influenced the election results at all. While the evidence is mixed, there is certainly no data that demonstrates that these techniques were able to change voting habits so that Cambridge Analytica helped US states 'turn red instead of blue', as claimed by their former director in the Netflix documentary The Great Hack.[44] The report concluded that we just do not know enough about the triggers for nudging voting behaviour to make such claims.

The consequence of all this is therefore both disturbing and reassuring at the same time. What Cambridge Analytica did to understand and target individuals using common state-of-the-practice approaches is accessible to all organizations and is happening to us all the time. The frequency of these attempts to influence us will increase, and their range will undoubtedly grow.

However, despite this, gaining advantage and influence from the use of this data has been found to be far more difficult than many had expected. While the targeting and focus for messaging was found to be quite precise, it was hard to understand impact and tracking it was poor. Additional attention to gain insight into the value of this microtargeting was clearly lacking.

Key lessons

Three broad lessons on personal data management for digital leaders emerge from the Cambridge Analytica scandal and the subsequent investigation.

- The case underscores the critical importance of transparency and the ethical use of AI and data analytics. The scandal involved the unauthorized gathering of vast amounts of personal data from Facebook users, highlighting the potential for misuse when data collection is not transparent or ethical. Digital leaders must prioritize transparency in data collection practices, ensuring users are informed about how their data is used and obtaining explicit consent. Ethics should be at the forefront of AI applications to prevent potential harm to individuals and society.

- Robust impact measurement and accountability frameworks are essential when implementing AI analytics. Despite the sophisticated use of AI by Cambridge Analytica, the investigation found a lack of clear evidence that their tactics significantly influenced election results. This highlights the importance of not just implementing AI technology but also measuring its impact accurately. Digital leaders should establish mechanisms for tracking and assessing the effectiveness of AI applications, ensuring accountability for their outcomes.

- The techniques used by Cambridge Analytica were not groundbreaking or unique; the company employed commonly available data science methods. This emphasizes that the capabilities of AI and data analytics are accessible to many organizations. Digital leaders should recognize that similar AI capabilities are within reach and are probably already employed by others. This awareness should drive a focus on continuous innovation and differentiation in AI use, as well as a commitment to understanding the broader landscape of AI applications to remain competitive and responsible.

As personal data management becomes a more widespread aspect of AI adoption, digital leaders can learn from the Cambridge Analytica case to prioritize transparency and ethics, establish robust impact measurement frameworks, and recognize the accessibility of AI capabilities. These lessons are essential for navigating the evolving landscape of AI in a responsible and effective manner.

Key questions and next steps

What is the best way of exploring AI adoption case studies from other sectors?

Review current literature and social medial channels to learn about AI adoption experiences across a wide range of sectors. Ask questions about the way those situations developed to relate them to your own contexts and situations. Form opinions about where and how their experiences could be relevant to you. When you see areas of special significance to your current challenges, investigate these case studies in more detail by following up with, making visits to or contacting those involved. Above all, keep an open mind and share your thoughts with colleagues and peers.

How can each sector's lessons be applied to other industries undergoing digital transformation?

Investigate the experiences of digital transformation in other industries such as the education and defence sectors. Establishing collaboration channels with tech companies, academia and other sectors can provide ways to gain valuable insights and accelerate the adoption of innovative technologies. Creating forums for knowledge exchange, participating in joint research initiatives and fostering partnerships with digital leaders from various domains will contribute to a more comprehensive understanding of digital transformation challenges and opportunities. Embracing a collaborative mindset will enable defence organizations to stay at the forefront of technological advances.

What do the lessons from the Cambridge Analytical scandal reveal about the challenges of personal data analytics?
Explore the core data science techniques in use in your organization. Review the potential issues in personal data management and prioritize transparency in data collection and usage. Ensure users know what data is being collected, how it is analysed and for what purposes. Focus on ethical data practices that build trust with users rather than manipulative tactics that might backfire.

Further reading

Davenport, Thomas H., and Steven M. Miller. 2022. *Working with AI: Real Stories of Human–Machine Collaboration.* MIT Press.

Lawry, Tom. 2022. *Hacking Healthcare: How AI and the Intelligence Revolution Will Reboot an Ailing System.* Productivity Press.

Marr, Bernard, and Matt Ward. 2019. *Artificial Intelligence in Practice: How 50 Successful Companies Used AI and Machine Learning to Solve Problems.* Wiley.

PART IV

DELIVERING VALUE FROM AI

CHAPTER 9

A responsible approach to AI

Everyone needs a basic understanding of AI to participate in discussions about its responsible development and deployment. Core to this are key principles for the ethical use of AI. All of us must take responsibility for learning about ways to make the use of AI appropriate, effective and fair for all.

Out of nowhere a new question has begun to dominate the business agenda: how can we control and govern the impact of AI on our future?

This is a critical concern given the shockwave induced by the latest wave of generative AI tools: ChatGPT, Gemini, Claude, and so on. Unfortunately, when we look for answers, we all too often find a series of banal statements about out-of-control autonomous decision making, unsupported claims about restrictions in trade, or privacy paranoia about the emergence of 'machines that think for themselves'. At best these discussions serve as provocations to ensure we examine the limits of the powerful technologies under development. At worst they are poorly informed speculation about an uncertain future based on little or no evidence.

Yet, beyond the futurology and the scare stories, leaders and decision makers are now required to participate in a key debate that is likely to have a deep effect on our understanding of AI and its adoption. It is a conversation dominated by three key concerns.

The first involves the human costs of AI. As AI is more widely adopted, its use impacts more and more people. We must face up to how these effects are managed in the short term and engage in the debate about how we maximize their benefits in the longer term. The second concern is in regard to the role of regulation in guiding and constraining what could, should and must be implemented by AI technology providers and consumers as they adopt AI in support of different business and societal needs. And the third involves a broader attempt to promote the concept of 'responsible AI'[1] and to encourage policymakers, leaders, practitioners and citizens to prioritize responsibility in all aspects of AI use.

The human costs of AI

Most people exploring AI adoption focus their attention on understanding the advanced technology that defines it. They are enamoured by the speed of its operation, its versatility and its sophisticated analytics. However, this focus can obscure an important factor: AI requires significant human effort. For instance, consider how the data used to train AI systems is acquired and processed.

A common reaction when people learn about the way that many of today's datasets are acquired, tagged and used goes something like: 'I always knew it was bad. But I didn't realize it was this bad.' Reports such as Josh Dzieza's article in The Verge describe the origins of the large datasets that feed AI systems and discuss the ways in which data is procured so that AI algorithms can be trained, tuned and tailored for particular tasks.[2] Dzieza's article outlines the enormous amount of manual effort that is required to optimize the algorithms at the heart of many kinds of AI approach and to build the large language models that drive generative AI tools such as ChatGPT and Gemini.

According to these reports, making machines appear to be human takes a remarkable number of people. They are needed to create the data sources that drive the AI algorithms and fuel the analytics used in decision making. As Dzieza says:

> You might miss this if you believe AI is a brilliant, thinking machine. But if you pull back the curtain even a little, it looks more familiar, the latest iteration of a particularly Silicon Valley division of labor, in which the futuristic gleam of new technologies hides a sprawling manufacturing apparatus and the people who make it run.

Such articles are a wake-up call and a reminder that in times of massive technological change, people suffer.[3] Sometimes a lot of people.[4] This is a troubling aspect of the digital transformation of business and society that all of us must face up to. With the recent acceleration of AI adoption, taking time to reflect both on the role of data in driving AI and on the dilemmas raised by advances in this technology is essential.

The humans in the loop

It is worth repeating that the secret to AI is people: humans and machines working together and supporting each other.[5] However, we also need to be aware of the potential negative impacts of this relationship. With increasing adoption of AI technologies, it is becoming clear that such interaction comes with a variety of troubling human costs.

- *Job displacement and reskilling.* Automation driven by AI can lead to the displacement of certain jobs, particularly those involving repetitive and routine tasks.[6] While AI creates new job opportunities in areas such as AI development, data analysis and AI ethics, the transition is hard on individuals whose skills become obsolete. Many people will struggle to adjust.

- *Bias and fairness concerns.* Biases and influences from many directions place pressure on the ways that AI systems are built and evolve. This can exacerbate existing inequalities and lead to discriminatory outcomes in areas like hiring, lending and law enforcement.[7]

- *Privacy and security.* AI technologies, particularly when used in the collection and analysis of personal data, raise significant privacy concerns.[8] The extensive collection and analysis of personal data for profiling and decision making can erode individual privacy rights and lead to unintended consequences, such as inappropriate monitoring and profiling.

- *Ethical dilemmas.* Deploying AI systems brings many kinds of ethical dilemmas to decision-making processes.[9] For instance, there are well-known case studies that highlight the issues faced when self-driving cars need to make split-second decisions that involve weighing different priorities to choose a 'least bad action'.[10] Determining the 'right' course of action in such situations is complex, ambiguous and open to ethical challenges.

- *Depersonalization of customer service.* The use of AI-powered chatbots and automated customer service systems can result in a depersonalized customer experience. While these technologies offer efficiency, they can be viewed as 'dehumanizing', lacking the empathy and nuanced understanding that human interactions provide.[11]

- *Mental health impact.* Constant connectivity, social media algorithms and AI-driven content recommendations have been linked to negative impacts on mental health.[12] These technologies can contribute to feelings of social isolation, lack of self-worth and addiction.

- *Loss of human judgment.* Overreliance on AI systems can lead to a decline in human judgment and critical thinking. From Nicholas Carr's warnings about 'Google making us stupid'[13] to more recent comments on the need for 'explainable AI',[14] blindly following technology-driven AI recommendations reduces individual participation in and understanding of complex situations and removes the need for people to learn how decisions are made.

It has always been about data

Beneath each of these human dilemmas is a story about data.[15] The way that AI systems procure, manage and apply data is a determining factor in the human–machine relationship. This raises its head most obviously in the way AI systems are trained.[16]

The quality and effectiveness of AI systems are intricately tied to the source and calibre of their training data.[17] Good training data is the foundation upon which AI models are built, shaping their capabilities, accuracy and real-world applicability. It serves as the essential raw material that allows AI algorithms to recognize patterns, make predictions and perform tasks with accuracy and relevance.[18]

In a rapidly advancing AI landscape, the importance of high-quality training data cannot be overstated. It is the cornerstone on which the entire AI infrastructure rests. Investments in obtaining and maintaining good training data pay off by yielding AI systems that provide accurate, reliable and valuable insights, ultimately determining the systems' success and impact across various industries and applications.

Training data essentially guides AI models in understanding the complexities of the world.[19] When the data is comprehensive, diverse and representative, the AI system can generalize from the examples it has seen during training to make informed decisions on new data. This capacity for generalization is what makes AI systems valuable and adaptable to different scenarios. Conversely, poor-quality or biased training data can lead to skewed outcomes and unreliable predictions.[20] The importance of good training data is particularly evident in supervised learning, where AI models learn from labelled examples.[21] If the labels are incorrect or inconsistent, the AI's understanding becomes flawed. In addition, the absence of specific examples can hinder the AI's ability to grasp the full scope of a task, limiting its performance.

However, obtaining good training data can be costly,[22] and it is also harder to come by than many people think.[23] Ensuring good training data involves meticulous curation, validation and augmentation. Data then needs to be cleaned, verified and balanced to mitigate biases and inaccuracies. Moreover, the continuous refinement of training data is vital to keep AI models up to date and relevant as trends and contexts evolve. As Dzeiza's *Verge* article reminds us, this takes people – a lot of people.[24] The latest AI advances illustrate just how much data is required. It is estimated that GPT-3.5, the LLM underlying OpenAI's ChatGPT, was trained on 570 GB of text data from the internet, which OpenAI says included books, articles, websites and social media.[25]

Let data be your guide

Regardless of the collection or generation process, the quality and volume of training data are critical factors that significantly influence the performance and reliability of AI models. There are three major concerns related to these aspects that affect responsible use of AI.

The first is *bias and unfairness*. One of the foremost concerns in this area is the presence of bias in training data.[26] If the training data is biased, the AI model will learn and then perpetuate those biases, potentially leading to discriminatory or unfair outcomes. Biases can arise from historical inequalities present in the data or from sampling biases that do not accurately represent the diversity of the real world. For instance, if a facial recognition system is trained predominantly on one demographic group, it might perform poorly on other groups, exacerbating existing societal biases.[27] Ensuring a diverse and representative dataset is crucial to mitigating bias and promoting fairness.

The second is *data quality and labelling*. The accuracy and reliability of the training data labels are paramount. Both incorrectly labelled data[28] and noisy data[29] can mislead an AI model and result in poor performance. In supervised learning, where models learn from labelled examples, even a small percentage of mislabelled data can have a significant negative impact.[30] Maintaining data quality requires careful validation, error correction and constant monitoring. In domains such as medical diagnosis or autonomous driving, unreliable labels can lead to serious consequences, making data quality a critical concern.[31]

The third is *data volume and generalization*. The volume of training data plays a crucial role in the ability of AI models to generalize.[32] Too much data might result in overfitting, where the model memorizes the training data but fails to perform well on new data. On the other hand, insufficient data can limit a model's ability to grasp the complexities of a task. While deep-learning models thrive on large datasets, collecting and annotating massive amounts of data can be time consuming and resource intensive.[33]

A multifaceted approach is required to address these concerns.[34] It involves careful data collection, preprocessing and augmentation to ensure a diverse and representative dataset. Implementing techniques for detecting and mitigating bias, in both data collection and model training, is crucial. Data quality control measures, such as crowd-sourced validation or expert reviews, can help maintain accurate labels.[35] Additionally, techniques such as transfer learning[36] can enable models to leverage knowledge from one domain to improve performance in another, even when data is limited.

Keeping it real

Dzieza's article reminds us that AI requires significant human effort to be effective. Behind the scenes, the success of AI hinges on something that is often overlooked: high-quality training data. Quality training data is the bedrock of AI's capabilities and the raw material that shapes AI models' accuracy, adaptability and real-world performance. However, it is often expensive and difficult to create and complex to manage, and it all requires a lot of people doing challenging work.

Furthermore, while AI offers tremendous benefits, it also presents significant challenges that demand our attention. Job displacement, bias, privacy concerns and ethical dilemmas are real issues that need careful consideration. In this era of rapid technological change, it is crucial to recognize this as part of the interplay between humans and AI.

As we embrace AI's potential, it is essential that we emphasize the importance of meticulous data curation, diverse representation and bias mitigation. By doing so, we can pave the way for AI systems that enhance our lives while upholding ethical and societal standards.

Regulating AI

Critical to the responsible use of AI and managing the data on which it relies is an emerging set of regulations aimed at ensuring that AI is applied fairly, appropriately and for the widest possible benefit. The role of regulation in governing the future of AI elicits a broad set of views and perspectives. The stakeholders' priorities and concerns vary enormously, from driving profitability for venture capital investors and Big Tech product providers through to protecting human rights and privacy for concerned citizens' rights groups, unions and workers' councils. Inevitably, senior leaders in both the public and private sectors find that they are at the forefront of grappling with how to navigate a path through the complex issue of AI regulation. Doing so requires balancing these opposing concerns in deciding where, how and why regulations can be meaningfully applied.

The question of 'where' to regulate hinges on balancing innovation with risk mitigation. Should oversight come from individual nations, international collaborations or a combination of both? Each approach offers advantages: national regulations can be tailored to specific needs, while international efforts can prevent a fragmented landscape that hinders responsible development.

'How' to regulate AI requires equally careful consideration. Again, striking the right balance is crucial. Overly prescriptive regulations could stifle progress, while lax controls could leave the door open for misuse. Senior leaders must consider focusing on principles like fairness, transparency and accountability, allowing flexibility for technological advancements. This might involve creating frameworks for bias detection in algorithms or establishing clear lines of responsibility for AI decision making.

Ultimately, the 'why' of AI regulation boils down to safeguarding public trust and well-being. AI has the potential to revolutionize public services, healthcare and infrastructure, but unchecked biases in algorithms could perpetuate discrimination, and autonomous systems raise concerns about safety and control. By establishing clear regulations, leaders can ensure responsible AI development that benefits society while minimizing potential harms.

The European Union's AI Act

The challenge being faced by senior leaders in addressing regulation of AI is illustrated quite dramatically by the EU AI Act.[37] After a long period of discussion and drafting, EU lawmakers gave final approval to the twenty-seven-nation bloc's artificial intelligence law in March 2024, putting the Act's world-leading rules on track to take effect later in 2024.

The EU AI Act is a comprehensive regulation that aims to ensure the responsible and ethical use of AI systems across the EU.[38] The Act applies to a wide range of stakeholders across the AI landscape, including technology providers, public sector bodies and businesses, regardless of where they are based in the EU. The Act establishes a risk-based approach, classifying AI systems into different risk categories based on their potential impact on users and society. High-risk AI systems are subject to more stringent requirements, while AI systems considered to pose an unacceptable risk are prohibited altogether. The Act also prohibits certain AI practices, such as manipulating human behaviour, exploiting people's vulnerabilities or social scoring based on personal characteristics.

The Act has significant implications for both businesses and consumers.[39] Businesses are required to ensure that their AI systems are safe, clear and respectful of their users. They must also comply with the Act's requirements, including due diligence obligations in the development of the AI system, mechanisms to verify the correctness of their decisions, and avenues to hold individuals accountable if a decision is found to be incorrect. Non-compliance with the AI Act can result in significant sanctions, including financial penalties and restrictions on the use of AI systems.

Consumers, on the other hand, can benefit from the Act's emphasis on transparency, accountability and ethical use of AI systems. The Act requires providers of AI systems to ensure that their systems are transparent, explainable and fair.[40] This means that consumers can better understand how AI systems make decisions and that they have more control over those systems' use.

The Act also has implications beyond the EU.[41] As the first comprehensive regulation of AI systems anywhere in the world, the Act is likely to set a global standard in this field – similar to the way in which the UK's General Data Protection Regulation, or GDPR, became a widely adopted data standard. This means both that businesses outside the EU will need to comply with the Act's requirements if they want to operate in Europe, and also that the Act could have additional ripple effects around the world. More broadly, in terms of the ongoing debate about AI regulation, the EU AI Act is a significant milestone. The Act is an important indication of how EU lawmakers view the balance that is required in ensuring AI's benefits are not outweighed by its pitfalls. It aims to ensure the responsible and ethical use of AI systems in the EU while also promoting innovation and competitiveness for companies operating in the bloc. Businesses and consumers can benefit from the Act's emphasis on transparency, accountability and ethical use of AI systems, but they must also comply with the Act's requirements if they want to avoid potentially significant sanctions.

As with all such regulations, a key hurdle for the EU AI Act is yet to come: its implementation and enforcement. Much of its utility depends on how the regulations are interpreted, executed and managed. For example, many organizations creating or using AI tools are already expressing concerns about the potential costs of compliance, while regulatory authorities charged with ensuring the Act is enforced worry about whether they have the necessary skills and resources to perform their tasks. This area is undoubtedly one that will receive substantial attention in coming months.

Elements of responsibility

Regulations such as the EU AI act form one thread of a much broader debate about the responsible use of AI. For some time, there have been criticisms of the biases embedded in AI,[42] of a lack of fairness in its algorithms,[43] and of the role of Big Tech companies in dominating the availability of AI systems.[44] These are serious concerns and they demand investigation and discussion. They form part of a much more deeply rooted unease with placing our trust in AI, as seen in recent surveys.

A recent UK National Audit Office study into the use of AI in government included a December 2023 survey of eighty-nine government bodies.[45] The report it produced is a 'value for money' assessment submitted to parliament to monitor ongoing actions on AI deployment and to provide input to future policy actions. The key finding from the study was that government agencies are in different stages of establishing a responsible approach to AI adoption. In practice, while some government bodies have begun implementing AI, widespread adoption is in its early stages and remains limited. The report highlights that achieving AI-at-Scale requires not only technological investment, but also significant changes to internal practices, external governance processes and workforce capabilities. Historically, meeting these needs has been found to be severely challenging in large-scale digital change programmes in UK government.[46] The study emphasizes that applying the lessons from these experiences will be important as the UK government drives its AI ambitions forward.

This point was also clearly highlighted as the fundamental takeaway from the latest IBM Global AI Adoption Index.[47] Conducted in April 2022, the study explores the deployment of AI across 7,502 businesses around the world and shows that a majority of organizations that have adopted AI have not yet taken key steps to ensure their AI is trustworthy and responsible. Nearly three-quarters (74%) of firms surveyed had not reduced unintended bias, 68% were not tracking performance variations and model drift, and 61% were not making sure they were able to explain AI-powered decisions.

Unsurprisingly, the IBM study points out that the challenges faced by many of these organizations to enhance responsibility is multifaceted. Addressing such concerns requires a coordinated approach that affects all those involved in the AI value chain, but two sets of participants are particularly affected.

• The first is the developers and engineers responsible for designing and implementing AI systems that must adhere to ethical standards and legal regulations. By incorporating transparency, fairness and accountability into AI algorithms, developers can mitigate biases and promote responsible decision making.

- And the second is the data scientists, who must be vigilant in recognizing and addressing potential biases in data that could result in discriminatory outcomes. Additionally, data scientists must strive for transparency and interpretability in their AI models to enable meaningful human oversight.

While helpful, this IBM study adopts an engineering perspective that must be aligned with the broader context in which AI is being used. Notably, many organizations and institutions are looking to establish a wider ethical framework that can be applied to guide their approach to AI. This has naturally been a priority for heavily criticised AI technology producers such as Microsoft,[48] Google[49] and IBM,[50] but it is also true of many other organizations, from the BBC[51] to the NHS.[52]

As an illustration, consider the ethical framework for AI use in the UK's defence sector published in June 2022.[53] This explicitly adopted a broad systems perspective to address a wide set of AI-related issues. Its scope is defined by five key principles.

- *Human-centricity.* The impact of AI-enabled systems on humans must be assessed and considered, and this must be done for a full range of effects, both positive and negative, across the entire system lifecycle.

- *Responsibility.* Human responsibility for AI-enabled systems must be clearly established, ensuring accountability for their outcomes, with clearly defined means by which human control is exercised throughout the systems' lifecycles.

- *Understanding.* AI-enabled systems, and their outputs, must be appropriately understood by relevant individuals, with mechanisms to enable this understanding made an explicit part of system design.

- *Bias and harm mitigation.* Those responsible for AI-enabled systems must proactively mitigate the risk of unexpected or unintended biases or harms resulting from these systems, whether through their original rollout or as the systems learn, change or are redeployed.

- *Reliability.* AI-enabled systems must be demonstrably reliable, robust and secure.

These five principles offer a useful basis for examining the range of effects of AI, and they create a great starting point for organizations and institutions to debate the way they should approach AI-based activities to ensure they are developed without bias, and that they are distributed fairly and deployed effectively.

The 'I' in AI

Common to these perspectives is a key point that must underpin any responsible approach to AI: responsible AI starts with you. As AI continues to advance, each of us must accept that we have a personal responsibility to learn more about the technology of AI, the human costs of AI adoption, and the broader societal impacts of its use.

The importance of this perspective can be clearly seen when observing discussions on the opportunities and challenges of AI in the workplace. It is typical to observe a very wide spread of knowledge of AI among those taking part in such discussions: while some have spent time learning about the technology and considering its implications, many have no meaningful base from which to draw conclusions.

Of course, not everyone can be – or needs to be – an expert in AI. It is a vast field of study with many avenues. However, to participate in the debate on how AI will impact our future, whether as a responsible leader, a manager, a product owner or a citizen, it has become essential to gain an appreciation for the basic concepts of the technology.

An illustration of the varying levels of understanding of AI can be obtained by asking people a simple question: what does GPT stand for in ChatGPT? Many will not have an answer, even if they use the system on a frequent basis. As a result, they are likely to have only a very limited understanding of how such a tool operates, which creates important barriers to its effective and responsible use.

Why does this matter? With broad agreement that AI is likely to have a significant impact on all our lives, it has become imperative that we arm ourselves with some basic vocabulary and concepts for engaging in meaningful discussion and effective use of AI. Calls for a more responsible approach to AI are urgent and important, but organizational structures and ethical frameworks will only be effective if each of us accepts our own personal responsibility to learn more about AI, to challenge ourselves to consider the ways in which AI is changing our world, and to adopt a more considered approach to the flurry of AI advances that will impact our work and lives.

Key questions and next steps

How can our organization align with principles of responsible AI and ensure ethical considerations are integrated into AI development and deployment?

Take a proactive role in aligning your organization with responsible AI principles. This involves fostering a culture of ethical AI development by working closely with developers and engineers. Establishing guidelines that prioritize transparency, fairness and accountability in AI algorithms is essential. Regular training and awareness programmes can ensure that teams are well versed in ethical considerations, enabling them to embed responsible practices into the entire AI development lifecycle. Additionally, organizations can contribute to industry-wide efforts to develop ethical frameworks and best practices to collectively advance responsible AI adoption.

How can we empower our workforce to understand the impact of AI and participate in responsible AI discussions?

Ensuring that the workforce is equipped to engage in meaningful discussions about AI's impact is crucial for responsible AI adoption. Initiate training programmes that teach employees basic AI concepts and vocabulary. This foundational knowledge will empower individuals to actively participate in conversations about AI's implications for their roles and for their organization as a whole. Encouraging a learning culture in which employees are motivated to stay informed about AI advancements and their potential impact will contribute to a more informed and responsible workforce.

What steps can be taken to address the challenges highlighted in AI adoption studies, such as biases, lack of transparency and accountability?

Collaborate with developers, data scientists and relevant stakeholders to establish clear protocols. These protocols should specifically target reducing unintended biases, tracking performance variations, ensuring transparency and enabling explanations for AI-powered decisions. By incorporating these measures into the AI development process, organizations can demonstrate their commitment to addressing critical issues in AI adoption. Regular audits and assessments should be conducted to measure progress and identify areas for improvement, ensuring continuous refinement of AI systems.

Further reading

Lu, Qinghua, Jon Whittle, Xiwei Xu and Liming Zhu. 2024. *Responsible AI: Best Practices for Creating Trustworthy AI Systems*. Addison-Wesley.

Veliz, Carisa. 2021. *Privacy is Power: Why and How You Should Take Back Control of Your Data*. Corgi.

Zuboff, Shoshana. 2019. *The Age of Surveillance Capitalism: The Fight for a Human Future at the New Frontier of Power*. Profile Books.

CHAPTER 10

Digital resilience for AI

Digital transformation brings constant change to all aspects of an organization. Addressing this requires resilience. The starting point for AI-driven transformation is to ensure data resilience. In addition, success requires adopting a six-point 'digital resilience' framework to address uncertainty and thrive in a rapidly evolving digital landscape.

Surrounded by the instability and uncertainty that is prevalent in many sectors of the digital economy, organizations are forced to accept that an ability to recognize and manage change is more important than ever. Many of these changes involve small adjustments to current ways of working. However, as organizations adopt digital technologies to improve their core operating processes, they also look to make more fundamental shifts across all their business activities. By encouraging a more disciplined approach to digital transformation, they seek longer-term systemic change aimed at revolutionizing the organization's structure, strategy, skills and systems.

For many organizations this is nothing new. To a large degree, all management is change management.[1] And as Robert Schaffer has argued, leaders should view change not as an occasional disruptor but as the very essence of their management job. However, traditional change management often considered change as being detached from 'normal' management tasks, treating it as a separate process that takes an organization from one stable state to another.[2] In digital transformation, where change is constant, such a perspective on change management can be very limiting. Instead, it must be considered the essence of management, with implications on all of an organization's activities.

Yet, it takes no more than a cursory review of large-scale digital transformation efforts to recognize that managing change is hard. Recent experiences such as those aimed at digitally transforming the UK's tax system[3] reveal that the struggle to stay on top of the broad impacts of change can overwhelm even the most well-designed strategies. How can organizations define a meaningful approach to change that allows them to adapt to current changes and prepare for the unexpected? An answer may be found by placing a fundamental focus on understanding and strengthening digital resilience.

Perspectives on digital resilience

Creating a strong plan is all very well. But, as often quoted, no plan survives first contact with the enemy.[4] Hence, resilience plays a critical role in the success of any digital strategy. In the context of digital transformation, it is this resilience that determines the ability of an organization to adapt, recover and thrive in the face of unexpected challenges, disruptions or changes in the digital landscape.

Its importance was highlighted throughout the Covid crisis, when companies that had invested in a robust digital infrastructure, cloud-based tools and secure remote access capabilities experienced smoother transitions to remote work setups and were able to continue serving customers and generating revenue.[5] Throughout those difficult times, the importance of resilience for business continuity was clear, and this has not diminished. In fact, it has grown with the continued pressure to find new ways of serving customer needs in an era disrupted by significant economic, political and financial instability. In December 2022 this was recognized by McKinsey in an extensive survey that showed that digital resilience was a priority for the majority of the organizations who responded.[6] Rapid deployment of solutions based on generative AI is only serving to increase this focus.[7]

But what does it mean to be resilient in the face of the kind of disruptive digital change we are experiencing with AI? The starting point for responding to this question is to examine the role of data as the foundation for AI. Data is the fuel for AI, and the utility of AI is directly related to the quality, accuracy and availability of that data. A resilient approach to the way data is gathered, stored, managed and maintained is essential.

Data resilience

Smarter approaches to data-driven decision-making require organizations to build the capabilities needed to bring together multiple data sources, filter out errors in the data, extract meaningful insights from repeated patterns, and so on. Establishing a broad approach to data resilience enables the data-driven insight at the heart of machine intelligence (MI).[8]

It is the combination of capabilities provided by MI that transforms so much data into genuine sources of new value. It can be seen as a core capability for the digital economy.[9] MI holds out the promise of being able to make sense of large volumes of data by exploiting a combination of machine learning and AI to yield entirely new sources of value. It encompasses natural language processing, image recognition, algorithmic design and other techniques to extract patterns, learn from these by assessing what they mean, and act upon them by connecting information together.

MI is inevitably disruptive by nature. Hence, it is essential to recognize that MI and its associated digital business models may pose significant challenges, which can be addressed in the following ways.

- *Changing the way data is collected and processed.* It is important to move away from localized databases associated with specific applications and form larger data lakes that can be exploited by new layers of intelligence essential to MI success.

- *Ensuring a flexible, scalable technology infrastructure across your organization.* Business success requires integrating the many applications that constitute a complex set of workflows by using open, component-based techniques as well as connected platforms such as those provided by AWS, Google, Microsoft, IBM and others.

- *Tackling cultural barriers across the organization.* Previous technology investment often constrained thinking and encouraged business leaders to cling on to ageing business models and supporting processes. New thinking is required.

While many of these changes will be ongoing, MI-based innovations will inevitably put stress on existing organizational structures. Leadership is always a critical element of any major organizational change, and until the key business leaders are convinced of the need for radical change, little progress will be made. Companies as diverse as major technology providers, large-scale business-to-consumer services providers and industrial business-to-business solutions providers are already seeing the impact of such changes, illustrating that effective progress can be made when the corporate culture is receptive to new ideas.

Further progress requires a clear plan. Business leaders and management should consider exploiting current technology-driven developments through three categories of activity: research, experimentation and execution. These three prongs are central to a robust data resilience strategy, and a range of different approaches to them are adopted by the most successful organizations: see below.

Research

- Familiarizing the organization with potential applications of MI-based digital technologies and considering where high-pay-off areas might be within the organization.

- Creating a clear map of the MI landscape as it affects the organization's view of the industries in which it competes, and examining new start-ups in their sector as early signals of market change.

- Examining new MI-based business models that could challenge the existing status quo or represent green-field opportunities.

Experimentation

- Engaging in open, honest discussions with their teams about the extent of data-driven decision making within the organization, and experimenting with new ways in which data could be obtained, curated and used.

- Conducting experiments or innovation sprints with appropriate partners to evaluate possibilities prior to scaling to identify minimum viable solutions.

- Engaging in small-scale pilot deployments of MI that focus on learning about the processes, skills and impact on the organization.

Execution

- Ensuring that key roles and functional areas in the organization are set up to act as appropriate entry points for MI-based innovations by engaging with start-ups and technology leaders (e.g. CTOs and CIOs).

- Creating time in projects to build stories around successes and failures that inspire and motivate teams to gain a shared understanding and vocabulary about MI and its supporting technologies.

- Promoting internal successes across the organization to highlight behaviours and approaches to MI that demonstrate progress in enhancing analytical capabilities and illustrate ways of working that the organization wants to encourage.

The six faces of resilience for AI

However important, data resilience on its own is insufficient. Digital transformation relies on a complex stack of technologies and practices to support change across the enterprise. In practice, we can identify an additional six distinct faces of resilience that must be addressed to ensure the success of delivering AI at scale.

1. *System resilience.* Architecting systems and solutions to be fault tolerant, adaptive and able to fail gracefully when operating incorrectly or compromised.

2. *Cyber resilience.* Ensuring that systems and data are protected from external threats and that information is exposed only through appropriate secure mechanisms.

3. *Information resilience.* Creating governance and management processes for data to ensure that all information is accurate, appropriate and responsibly sourced.

4. *Organizational resilience.* Establishing management and decision-making practices that enable rapid actions to be taken while conforming to all necessary laws, standards and guidelines.

5. *Operational resilience.* Continuing to perform as expected as the operating environment changes, systems are degraded or stakeholder demands expand.

6. *People resilience.* Supporting all employees and other stakeholders to perform at their best in the short term while sustaining their health and well-being over the longer term.

All six of these perspectives on resilience are important considerations, and together they form a framework for organizations to review their ability to manage change and sustain high performance in the context of the kinds of digital transformation that are being experienced with AI. While other digital resilience frameworks focus on one or other of these perspectives,[10] bringing these six angles together provides a more holistic view. Taking in the broader picture is essential in the age of AI.

Bend, don't break

Based on such experiences, there are many ways in which resilience is found to be central to a successful digital strategy. To improve how digital transformation activities can become more resilient to change, the six perspectives listed above can be used to ask five key questions of a digital strategy.

How prepared are we to adapt to change?

The digital landscape constantly evolves, with new technologies, market trends and customer expectations emerging all the time. A resilient digital strategy enables organizations to quickly adapt to these changes by being flexible, agile and responsive. It allows businesses to seize new opportunities, reorganize resources to adapt to changing circumstances, and mitigate risks effectively.

How well do we manage the risks associated with change?

Resilience helps organizations identify and manage the risks associated with their digital initiatives. This includes assessing potential vulnerabilities, implementing robust security measures, and establishing backup plans in case of disruptions such as cyber attacks, system failures or natural disasters. A resilient digital strategy considers risk mitigation as an integral part of its implementation.

What processes do we have in place to ensure continuity and recovery from disruptions?

Resilience ensures business continuity by enabling an organization to recover swiftly from disruptions. It involves having backup systems and redundancies in place to minimize downtime, data loss or customer impact. A resilient digital strategy incorporates disaster recovery plans, backup solutions and proactive monitoring to swiftly address any disruptions and restore normal operations.

Where can we improve customer trust and satisfaction in how we manage change?

Resilience is crucial for maintaining customer trust and satisfaction across all digital channels. When organizations provide uninterrupted services or products to their customers, it enhances their reputation and fosters customer loyalty. Resilience ensures that customer expectations are met even during unforeseen circumstances, which is crucial in today's interconnected and competitive digital landscape.

How do we encourage positive change to drive innovation and growth?

Resilience empowers those within an organization to experiment and innovate, and to pursue digital transformation initiatives with confidence. It encourages a culture of learning from failures and setbacks, fostering a mindset of continuous improvement. A resilient digital strategy promotes exploration of new technologies, business models and opportunities for growth while enabling organizations to recover quickly from any setbacks along the way.

A resilient approach to digital transformation

With no end in sight to the disruption and uncertainty we face in today's digital economy, resilience is an essential component of every successful digital strategy. It enables organizations to navigate uncertainties, adapt to change, manage risks, maintain continuity, build customer trust and foster innovation. As adoption of AI accelerates, ensuring data resilience is an essential first step. In addition, digital strategies must be tested against at least seven perspectives on resilience: data, system, cyber, informational, organizational, operational and people. By incorporating resilience into digital initiatives, organizations can position themselves for long-term success in a rapidly evolving digital landscape.

Key questions and next steps

How prepared are we to adapt to change, and how do we become more change-ready?

To enhance adaptability, foster a culture of continuous learning and agility within your organization. Conduct regular assessments of the digital landscape, keeping abreast of emerging technologies, market trends and evolving customer expectations. Encourage cross-functional collaboration and provide training programmes that equip teams with the skills needed to navigate change effectively. By embedding adaptability into the organizational culture, leaders can ensure a proactive response to evolving digital dynamics.

How can we improve the way we manage risk and improve resilience in AI adoption?

Effective risk management is foundational to resilience when adopting AI. Institute comprehensive risk assessments for digital initiatives, identifying potential vulnerabilities and implementing robust security measures. Develop and regularly update contingency plans to address disruptions, including cyber threats, system failures and natural disasters. By integrating risk mitigation strategies into their digital strategy, organizations can proactively safeguard against potential challenges.

What processes are important to have in place to ensure continuity and recovery from disruptions?

Resilience in the face of disruptions requires meticulous planning. Establish clear processes for business continuity and swift recovery. Implement backup systems, redundancies and disaster recovery plans to minimize downtime and data loss. Proactive monitoring tools should be in place to quickly detect disruptions and initiate recovery procedures. A well-defined continuity and recovery framework ensures that an organization can withstand unexpected challenges and maintain uninterrupted operations.

How do we enhance resilience to encourage positive change to drive innovation and growth?

Resilience empowers organizations to embrace positive change and drive innovation. Cultivate a culture that encourages experimentation and learning from failures. Establish mechanisms for continuous improvement and recognize and reward innovative initiatives. Provide resources and support for teams to explore new technologies and business models. A resilient digital strategy not only navigates disruptions but also stimulates a culture of innovation, propelling the organization towards sustainable growth.

Further reading

Leeson, William. 2023. *Data Engineering and AI for Beginners: Revolutionizing Data Processing and Analytics by Leveraging Artificial Intelligence for Efficient Input Collection, Storage, and Transformation.* Independently published.

Reiss, Joe, and Matt Housley. 2023. *Fundamentals of Data Engineering: Plan and Build Robust Data Systems.* O'Reilly.

CHAPTER 11

The role of AI in innovation

For many people, AI brings capabilities that drive a new approach to innovation based on using data-driven insights to learn and adapt quickly. Yet, innovation is more than just technology. A well-structured approach is needed to redefine innovation in terms of its feasibility, desirability and viability to create social and economic value. Digital leaders adopting AI must place it in the context of a well-defined innovation process.

I magine that you are walking down the aisle of your local supermarket looking to fill your shopping cart with your weekly groceries. As you make your way past the packed shelves, the price that you see for each item changes. What is displayed is calculated dynamically based on a variety of factors including your typical buying habits, what is already in your cart, the stock on hand in the warehouse, the discount offers being promoted by suppliers, the sell by dates of the currently displayed items, and perhaps several other concerns. This personalized pricing happens for others too, so that the person walking three paces behind you may well be charged a different amount for the same items you selected.

Is this technically feasible? Is it legal? Is it right? Is it what you want? Will this encourage you to buy more?

These are the kinds of scenario being envisaged by innovators and futurists as they think about AI and the future of retail, banking, education, entertainment and many other activities we carry out every day. Increasing digital transformation in these sectors has allowed them to consider many such possibilities. They push the boundaries about what is possible and what is not. By working through these kinds of exercises, innovators can consider what capabilities are provided by the latest technology advances, how clients behave in different situations, what kinds of experiences they value, and where additional investment can increase profitability for companies looking to move forward. In this environment, innovation requires a complex, multidimensional perspective. How can innovation be reinvented for the AI age?

Back to basics

Before looking forwards toward new approaches, consider the challenges faced in innovation and the role it plays in organizational strategy. Many authors have provided insights into the innovation process and explored the elements of innovation that are critical to success. Far from the misleading 'mad scientist' image of innovation, they emphasize that a vast majority of innovation requires a coordinated team executing a well-structured, disciplined approach. For instance, Peter Drucker, one of the most influential scholars in the field of management theory, highlighted that innovation is not an isolated activity but part of a broader collaborative value-creation process.[1] Here is his definition of innovation:[2]

> The effort to create purposeful, focused change in an enterprise's economic or social potential... The means by which the entrepreneur either creates new wealth-producing resources or endows existing resources with enhanced potential for creating wealth.

Several aspects of Drucker's definition are worth highlighting. First, the goal of innovation is purposeful change with an economic or societal impact. It is the outcome of innovation that guides and dictates the parameters of its success. Second, it is not only the resulting product or service that is important to innovation, but also the approach taken to get there. Innovation is as much about process as it is about ideas. Significantly, Drucker sees the process of innovation as a set of activities providing the basis for a systematic approach that organizations can take to be successful. Third, the actor in innovation – an entrepreneur – aims to make a financial or societal difference through his or her actions. Hence, the characteristics, experiences and personality of the entrepreneur play a key role in innovation.

Drucker's definition was given some years ago, and its perspective frames the role of innovation in relation to wealth creation through a coordinated, well-managed process. In the digital era, this remains an essential perspective on how an organization generates value.[3]

The changing context for innovation

While many of these fundamental ideas regarding innovation were developed some years ago, they are just as important to us today in the age of AI. A core aspect of any digital transformation is to establish a climate that encourages, rewards and supports innovation. In transforming large established organisations (LEOs) with complex structures and constraints, this is particularly critical – and also difficult to achieve.[4] Taking lessons from successful Silicon Valley start-ups can be helpful,[5] but it is not sufficient to ensure they can overcome the challenges of scale, complexity and inertia frequently experienced in many LEOs.

Experience from large-scale digital programmes has raised many questions about the way innovation is approached today. Are traditional innovation practices effective in today's fast-paced, volatile, digitally driven environment? What are the issues for LEOs as they establish their innovation climate? Certainly, much of the basis for innovation culture remains unchanged. However, several additional areas are worth emphasizing as critical to establishing a positive innovation culture in the age of AI. These include the following.

- *Highlighting the challenges and opportunities that require new ways of working.* Large-scale change demands a way of creating the required innovation momentum across an LEO. There must be compelling reasons to act to make it clear to leaders and managers that taking on the risks associated with new approaches is essential. Also, an LEO must ensure that the environment is such that if those risks are taken and updates do not work out as planned, people will not be worried about being punished. Honesty and transparency are vital here. First, about accepting that there is risk involved in innovation. Second, about how the risks of trying new, unproven ideas are viewed within the organization. And third, in recognizing that a level of 'psychological safety' is a prerequisite for taking on the challenges that come with trying out new ways of working in an LEO.

- *Introducing practical techniques for exploring new ideas, testing them in realistic scenarios, and defining meaningful approaches to their adoption.* The technical, business and human aspects of innovation must be addressed with methods and tools that help to apply them, measure their impact and quickly drive them towards adoption or rejection. It is not that people in LEOs do not know what can be done. Many such approaches exist. But they need a disciplined framework in which to apply this innovation. Unbounded innovation sounds good in theory, but in LEOs there need to be managed innovation channels or pathways to guide innovators and innovative ideas.

- *Creating adoption models and pathways that overcome innovation barriers.* Any entrepreneur inside an LEO understands that coming up with good ideas is a small part of the challenge they face. The biggest issues are trying to move from a workable initial solution to broader adoption in an organization that has built up many layers of resistance to change. Clear approaches to manage the scaling of innovative ideas are essential. These pathways to adoption need to be defined, managed and illustrated with explicit support from many agencies across the organization. Escalation processes are important when blockages occur because all too often good ideas are simply abandoned as the innovators become overwhelmed, frustrated and disillusioned.

- *Adapting to the organization's history and environment.* The earlier history and experiences with innovation in an LEO raise issues that must be addressed when working within a highly structured, complex environment. Any change agent in such a context will spend a large part of their time looking beyond current innovation challenges to assess previous attempts to overcome the inertia, organizational complexity, domain-specific regulations, financial controls and other concerns typical of such an environment. While general techniques can be useful, deeper knowledge of one's organization and its context are required to make significant progress.

- *Bringing insights from deep knowledge of the domain.* Measuring innovation culture through a general maturity framework provides a useful starting point to define the innovation journey. However, it must be refined with local knowledge of the domain, the market conditions, the competitive environment and current macroeconomic events. This is particularly important in light of AI's disruptive impact on business and society. Practices, priorities and processes for innovation that seemed relevant just a few months ago may now be obsolete. Known barriers to innovation from the past may today seem trivial. Prioritizing contemporary concerns is essential.

- *Recognizing the unique digital drivers for change.* Digital advances in the past decade have brought new opportunities and challenges to innovation. While it might seem easy to dismiss these as incremental ways to 'go faster', there are more fundamental aspects to consider. The digital world is ushering in a new era. We are seeing a massive jump in technical feasibility, with advances in AI, machine learning, pervasive high-speed communications and more. At the same time, diverse approaches to business viability are emerging. Innovative business models are creating new ways to capture value throughout the delivery process by taking advantage of real-time product usage data. Finally, client expectations are on the rise. Customers are increasingly willing to share personal data in real time from various embedded sensors in devices such as mobile phones. As a result, the ongoing digital revolution is changing innovation culture and approaches in critical, substantive ways.

Toward a golden age for digital innovation

Indeed, it could be argued that today's innovation opportunities are greater than ever before. In this age of AI, advances in the capabilities of digital technology have been aligned with major improvements in financial, cultural, regulatory and organizational domains to encourage entrepreneurship in all its forms. The current era, grounded in a broadening of digital skills and capabilities, provides the basis for rapid, low-cost experiments that are driving a wide range of new products and services.

Capitalizing on highly capable computer processors and the massive growth of new data sources, computing's focus has moved from the manipulation of data towards better ways of understanding and learning from that data in order to predict future behaviour. Andrew McAfee and Eric Brynjolfsson refer to this new focus as the 'second machine age'.[6] They argue that the changes underway in a digital world are as profound as those brought forth by the Industrial Revolution in the late eighteenth century.

The first machine age of the early twenty-first century was characterized by the deployment of digital technologies to optimize existing tasks through increased automation and open access to knowledge. In contrast, the second machine age we now occupy has advanced to a stage where AI-powered machines are capable of learning, connecting and reconfiguring their ways of working in light of past experiences. They adapt to changing circumstances. Machines can use the large amounts of data they examine to extract patterns that are then used to adapt their behaviours to look for new patterns, enabling them to predict future events.

However, as McAfee and Brynjolfsson emphasize, technological advances are only part of the equation. The second machine age is also driven by two additional trends that are beyond the growing core capabilities and capacity of machines: the appearance of large and influential young companies disrupting incumbents across numerous business domains, and the ability for organizations to tap into the energy and resources of large communities that are providing knowledge, expertise and drive.

Organizations seeking to be successful in the second machine age are beginning to recognize that adopting digital technologies is only part of the necessary strategy. Also critical to their future sustainability is an innovation-driven process that encourages a deeper analysis of the value they offer in a quickly evolving market; a broad examination of how they position their business activities in light of new entrants; and a careful review of their management practices to speed up decision making, establish appropriate levels of governance and motivate a workforce driven by new expectations and concerns. Such activities we now consider to be the essence of a 'digital transformation'.

As much as this transformation consists of modernization in technology, it is also a change of attitude and approach to innovation spawning new business practice and structures. Yet the question arises as to whether and how this wave of change can make a substantial impact on organizations slowed down by their scale, heritage and complex decision-making structures. Many recent surveys across different communities point towards the same conclusion: while business leaders recognize the importance and inevitability of digital transformation in their own organization and throughout their industry, few believe they themselves have a sufficient grasp of the core elements that shape such a transformation. This dichotomy is repeatedly highlighted across areas such as marketing, customer service delivery, governance, IT and management strategy.

Building from Brynjolfsson and McAfee's observations, we may also see the age of AI as extending the second machine age towards a new phase in our economic story. Carlota Perez holds that 'the sequence technological revolution–financial bubble–collapse–golden age–political unrest recurs about every half century and is based on causal mechanisms that are in the nature of capitalism'.[7] Given her view that the information age began in the 1970s and has dominated economics ever since, it seems appropriate that the current AI technology wave may well be the trigger that effectively starts the 'digital age' for all organizations.

The question, then, is where we see ourselves in this sequence of technological revolution–financial bubble–collapse–golden age–political unrest, and whether the digital revolution currently being experienced with the rise of AI will face the same fate as the previous five revolutions she identifies. Time will tell.

For now, we can accept that we live in a world where our approach to innovation is redefined based on values that are rapidly being reset in light of a range of issues, including concerns about technology's impact on the environment, the emergence of AI driven by several dominant Big Tech companies, China's role as a digital superpower, the changing world demographic profile, and the ongoing fallout from the global pandemic. In such a context, it is appropriate to rethink the role of innovation in an age of AI.

Redefining digital innovation

As a key concept that has received increasing attention[8] in recent years, innovation in a digitally disrupted world is often too narrowly defined in terms of technological invention or digitization of features in existing systems. With the wider implications of digital adoption in mind, a much broader perspective is required in the age of AI. The capabilities (or affordances) brought by digital solutions are important, but only when considered in the context of how they change our understanding of the tasks we carry out and the relationships among all the stakeholders involved.

To explore these issues, it is useful to reinterpret innovation within a well-used model that highlights the importance of ensuring an alignment of three critical components.

- *Feasibility.* The initial inspiration for innovators is often a new technological breakthrough. This brings fresh approaches to problem solving when digital solutions are used to replace existing manual and analogue approaches with digital alternatives. R&D labs and innovation accelerators are now filled with digital technology specialists testing out ranges of products and prototypes to explore the enhanced capabilities they provide. They move them through the technology readiness levels,[9] from idea to scaled working solution. At any one time, dozens of different technology-focused projects will be in flight.

- *Desirability.* Successful innovation solves a problem that matters to a customer. Whether the customers are internal or external, any innovation must address a problem that someone cares about, and it must provide a solution deployed in a way that the customer can readily consume. Digital solutions bring opportunities to gather data that was previously unavailable, inaccessible and uncoordinated. This opens up opportunities for greater insight into the challenges customers face. But knowing more does not mean that we understand how individuals and communities behave, the way they think, how they are influenced, or what kinds of new service they might value. Much greater attention is required to dig below the surface. Not only does this lead to efforts to know more about customers through increased customer analytics,[10] but it also sees innovators turning to areas such as ethnography and anthropology for more rigorous approaches to learning about human behaviour.[11]

- *Viability.* Much of the excitement surrounding new digital technologies is only justified if it can be exploited within a sustainable financial model that is appropriate to the operating context and constraints of the organization involved. Whether this is a start-up, an existing company or some other institution, a viable business model is essential. Digital technology advances have encouraged new business model alternatives, in particular allowing new ways to consolidate supply and demand for goods and services via platform-based approaches.[12] Even so, for a solution to be successful – even a digital one – a myriad of viability issues must be considered, including cost of production, strategic fit, impact on market and ecosystem, environmental impact and maintainability.

From here to infinity … and beyond

With the increasing sophistication of AI, it is easy to be seduced by its technological capabilities without adequately considering its broader role and effect. In a digital world it is essential to be reminded that innovation must be considered by looking beyond the technology. It involves the whole process, from opportunity identification to idea creation, from solution realization to prototyping, from production to marketing and sales. Furthermore, in a digital economy, delivering impact through innovation requires the capacity to quickly adapt to changing conditions and to the complex context faced by organizations and institutions as they evolve to adopt digital ways of working.

In this way, the impact, mindset and culture of innovation is seen to play a significant role in technology evolution. In an age of disruptive AI this broader perspective on innovation is essential to guide all organizations, industry bodies and government agencies to adopt an innovation approach that supports the alignment of three aspects: technical feasibility, user desirability and financial viability. From this more holistic perspective, digital innovation is a societal concern, not a technological one. It arises from the intersection of invention and insight, aimed at the creation of social and economic value. Its significance is critical for all of us.

Key questions and next steps

How can we enhance innovation by aligning technological feasibility with customer desirability and financial viability?

The intersection of technological innovation, customer needs and sustainable business models is crucial for success. Establish interdisciplinary teams that bring together technology specialists, customer experience experts and business strategists. Encourage collaboration between research and development labs, customer analytics teams and financial experts to ensure that innovations not only leverage the latest digital solutions but also address problems that are relevant to customers. Adopt approaches from disciplines such as anthropology to gain a deeper understanding of human behaviour, aligning technology initiatives with the genuine needs and desires of the target audience.

How do we redefine innovation in the context of the broader societal values and challenges emerging in the age of AI?

Innovation should not be confined to technological break-throughs; it must be viewed as a societal endeavour. Consider the broader impact of innovation on societal values, environmental concerns and evolving demographics. Engage in a dialogue with stakeholders, industry bodies and government agencies to redefine the role of innovation in the context of societal values. Encourage a mindset shift within your organization, so that innovation is viewed as a collaborative process aimed at creating social and economic value. Emphasize the importance of innovation beyond isolated events, considering the entire lifecycle from idea creation to societal impact.

How can we ensure that digital innovation with AI is adaptive to changing conditions and organizational contexts?

In the dynamic digital economy, adaptability is a key factor in successful innovation. Foster a culture that values adaptability and embraces change. Implement agile methodologies and frameworks that facilitate quick adjustments to evolving conditions. Encourage continuous learning and experimentation, recognizing that failure is a part of the innovation process. Establish mechanisms for cross-functional collaboration to address the complex challenges faced by organizations adopting digital ways of working. By embedding adaptability into the organizational culture, digital leaders can ensure that innovation remains responsive to changing contexts.

Further reading

Amit, Rafael, and Christopher Zott. 2021. *Business Model Innovation Strategy: Transformational Concepts and Tools for Entrepreneurial Leaders*. John Wiley & Sons.

Brynjolfsson, Erik, and Andrew McAfee. 2016. *The Second Machine Age: Work, Progress, and Prosperity in a Time of Brilliant Technologies*. W. W. Norton & Company.

Drucker, Peter. 2007. *Management Challenges for the 21st Century*. Routledge.

Perez, Carlota. 2003. *Technological Revolutions and Financial Capital: The Dynamics of Bubbles and Golden Ages*. Edward Elgar.

CHAPTER 12

Leading AI-at-Scale

There are many leadership challenges involved in adopting AI and digitally transforming an organization. To address them, leaders must balance top-down management styles with agile approaches that empower teams and speed up decision making. A blended approach must be defined that matches these ambitions with an organization's specific needs and context.

As organizations seek to make use of AI tools, a topic that generates a great deal of discussion and debate is the best way to adapt the role of leadership. How do leaders get the best out of their teams while adopting new digital technologies, encouraging innovation and experimentation, and driving a coordinated strategy to meet the organization's goals? How does AI change the way leaders review progress, make decisions and deliver value?

Recognizing, addressing and resolving this fundamental leadership dilemma is essential if an organization is to move beyond using digital technology to paper over the cracks in the organization's current ways of working and head towards a digital-first operating model that is essential to future success.

Yet, holding up the handful of agile-driven organizations as exemplars of the new way to work in the age of AI can be misleading. Fuelled by stories about companies such as Netf-lix[1] and Spotify,[2] many people are energized by the emphasis they see on flattened management structures,[3] rapid redirec-tion[4] and self-organized teams[5] empowered to make decisions for themselves in response to their local knowledge. They cel-ebrate an end to the days of being told what to do by out-of-touch managers who insist on everyone being forced to use the same out-of-date tools and methods regardless of the context.

However, for others responsible for scaling, coordinating and aligning an organization across its many strands, the agile prac-tices that are considered fundamental to digital transformation programmes are portrayed as an absence of leadership, an abdication of responsibility by those in management roles, and a disregard for the importance of the experiences gained from a lifetime of hard-earned lessons in delivering value to clients.[6] They see such moves as a threat to stability, a sign of disrespect for the hard-won skills of management, and a misunderstanding of the importance of maintaining strong governance across a diverse, complex organizational landscape.[7]

For organizations facing increasing digital disruption driven by AI, how can these extreme perspectives be reconciled? What are the critical areas for leadership in such an environment? Where should they focus their efforts to address the tensions being created by this leadership dilemma?

Reflections on recent leadership experiences

A useful starting point is to consider the 'great digital accelera-tion' that we witnessed over the challenging period of the recent global pandemic.[8] Rapid deployment of digital technology was essential to the survival of many organizations. A new accord was required to rethink risk profiles based on the need to move at speed and adapt rapidly to a changing environment while ensuring appropriate resilience, coordination and governance across all stakeholders. In reflecting on this experience, we find that there is much we can learn about leaders and leadership in times of disruptive change. The successful deployment of advanced digital technologies during that time was widely applauded.[9] Yet, at the same time, the disruptive forces unleashed raised broader concerns about how organizations and individuals must change to absorb the impact of their adoption.[10] In the rush towards digitization, digital transformation highlighted several areas of tension as the aspirations for technology-driven changes clashed with the reality of managing shifts in working practices. In such circumstances, ensuring meaningful, sustained impact became extremely challenging. This was particularly true in the complex world emerging from the covid crisis.

Adapting to such dramatic changes, one of the most challenging areas for many individuals was rethinking the role and the skills they required to lead their teams during this period.[11] Existing ways of organizing, managing and leading were found to be wanting. For organizations as a whole, the nature of leadership and of current ways to incentivize leaders' behaviour were cast into doubt.

From these considerations, a range of questions began to emerge that are extremely relevant in today's era of AI-driven disruption. What is the best way to encourage greater experimentation and risk taking from leaders during times of rapid change? How is the experience and expertise of leaders best used to drive digital transformation? How do additional automation and adoption of data-driven algorithms shift the focus of decision making away from those in leadership roles? What are the implications of AI and other digital shifts for organizational structures and career development?

The challenge of leadership

There are growing expectations that the accelerated adoption of digital technologies we saw during the pandemic will continue indefinitely. The arrival of new waves of AI capabilities only serves to reinforce this view. To ensure recovery and fuel growth following the pandemic, many believe that it is essential to maintain the speed at which these technologies are replacing manual practices and transforming business models towards digital-by-default engagement with clients.[12] This pressure has caused a significant shift in the attitudes and mentality of senior executives. In many cases these key decision makers have recognized for the first time the importance of their role in leading the digital transformation journey.

Attention is consequently turning to the nature of leadership in a digitally transformed organization and to the skills therefore required for success. Meaningful digital transformation at scale involves coordinating a wide range of activities at all levels of an organization. This is complex enough for leaders in these organizations. However, what makes this task even more difficult is that the fundamental principles and practice of leadership for digital transformation are being questioned.[13] Leaders wanting to drive meaningful, sustained organizational change must develop new skills and prioritize unfamiliar aspects of their strategy to achieve success.

So, what are the most effective characteristics of digital leaders? An obvious place to start is to look at the leadership traits of executives at successful digital native organizations. For these digital leaders, strategy and decision making have adapted to recognize that traditional top-down hierarchical models are unlikely to be effective in times of rapid change and massive uncertainty.[14] They base their leadership approaches on agile management principles aimed at rapid innovation cycles, experimentation to learn quickly from low-cost investments, and devolved decision making to speed up reaction times when the operating context changes.

Yet, while these characteristics are readily identified, the leadership approaches in many large established organizations remains stuck in the past. The incumbent bureaucratic approach to leadership developed during the industrial age emphasized the importance of productivity and efficiency through standardization and rigour. Hierarchical management models helped to organize large teams into manageable units aimed at achieving a common purpose through adherence to shared processes, where the steps to be taken are well rehearsed and the outcomes well known. While these models were well matched to previous ways of working, many see them as ineffective in digitally driven scenarios, where diversity, creativity and fast responses are highly prized.[15]

To overcome these limitations, organizations are looking to new leadership models. For example, in data-intensive domains typical of the age of AI, one potential direction is to accelerate access to new knowledge by building organizations based on meritocracy.[16] These data-driven organizations would perform detailed analysis and amass expertise to guide informed choices about future directions. Strategic decision making would be based primarily on evidence drawn from data. Those that master the data-driven technologies and their application would rise to the top. It is an approach that holds significant appeal for those looking to drive innovation across the organization. However, as we saw in responding to the Covid pandemic, this approach relies on attracting a core of digitally skilled employees and building a consistent base of meaningful data to which standard data analytics can be applied[17] – something that can be hard to achieve in these unprecedented times.

So, while this approach has helped many organizations in domains where digital change is well underway and where the goals are relatively predictable, it has been found to be suboptimal in many digital transformation situations characterized by massive uncertainty and a fast-changing environment. Here, the focus must necessarily be on speed of reaction to the weak signals received, with strategic intuition and opportunistic risk-taking playing a more significant role in leadership. This opportunistically focused approach, defined by Julian Birkinshaw and others as 'adhocracy', requires a fast-paced experimental learning cycle that thrives on uncertainty.[18] Leaders ensure progress by creating tightly integrated multidisciplinary teams focused on exploratory techniques such as short sprints and minimal viable products. Success with this approach requires a culture and a working environment that support the kind of dynamic delivery style this creates.

The politics of AI

However, leadership in the age of AI is about much more than worrying over internal management styles and organizational structures. While many of the headlines about AI focus on delivering software faster,[19] generating more lifelike images[20] or improving long-range weather forecasting,[21] it is easy to forget that there are some much bigger issues at stake here. Digital leaders and decision makers must recognize that the increased use of AI brings important responsibilities over why, where and how it is used effectively, efficiently and ethically.

At the heart of these concerns is a deeper understanding of how digital data is being gathered, managed, shared and exploited. Harnessing AI, and the data that feeds it, requires new leadership skills. To be effective, all digital leaders need a clear understanding of how data is collected, managed and used in AI applications; how organizations leverage it to influence behaviour; and how these forces play out in critical areas such as climate change, education and healthcare.

When nations collide

As we are all beginning to appreciate, AI will be an important part of our future. But what role will it play? From a national and international perspective, the rhetoric surrounding AI is fraught with tension. Anxieties over geopolitical competition and the widening digital divide are raising concerns about weaponization and manipulation of AI for political power.[22] This is seen in comments by US President Biden that the decisions being made on AI today will 'shape the direction of the world for decades to come'.[23] And it is echoed in China's President Xi Jinping's stated aim to control the use of AI as a core part of delivering the country's technical strategy[24] – and in the challenges he may face if he fails to get this right.[25]

At this level, we appear to be experiencing a renewed struggle for digital technological dominance.[26] China and the United States are engaged in a fierce tug-of-war over the future of AI, each driven by ambitious national agendas but with differing ethical perspectives.[27] China, with its centralized data landscape and focus on rapid progress, prioritizes economic and military applications, raising concerns about surveillance and privacy.[28] The United States, meanwhile, is worried about erosion of individual rights and democratic values,[29] advocating for open collaboration and responsible development. As both countries invest heavily in research and development, jockeying for talent and intellectual property, the rest of the world is left to wonder which direction AI will ultimately take and how it will impact the AI technology roadmap and the values that will govern how AI is adopted.

Important as these concerns are, they must be viewed as part of a much deeper debate that is taking place about the power of AI and how it should be applied responsibly at all levels of business and society. This is not an issue to be addressed only at the global geopolitical level. AI is rapidly transforming the world around us, promising unprecedented efficiency, personalized experiences and even solutions to global challenges. But beneath the glossy sheen of AI's potential lies a complex, and often murky, set of choices that need to be made, where data becomes power, algorithms drive constant surveillance and ethical considerations clash with pragmatic realities.

Data: the fuel of AI's political engine

The foundation of AI is data: vast, interconnected networks of information that power algorithms, train models and shape the outcomes of AI systems. Data is not neutral.[30] It reflects the biases, inequalities and power dynamics of the world in which it was collected. When used unquestioningly, AI can perpetuate these biases, leading to discriminatory outcomes in areas such as loan approvals, job applications, access to government services and even criminal justice.[31] The Cambridge Analytica scandal, where voter data was used to try to manipulate election outcomes, stands as a stark reminder of the potential for AI to be weaponized through biased and selective approaches to data use.[32]

All data is political

The extent to which seemingly objective and factual data is inherently intertwined with power dynamics, societal values and ideological perspectives is widely debated.[33] Indeed, leading technologists such as James Mickens at Harvard argue that all data science is political.[34] This is a result of several characteristics of data and its use.

- *Perspective and bias.* Data collection is not impartial; it is often influenced by the interests, beliefs and objectives of those gathering it. What is collected, how it is interpreted and the context in which it is presented can reflect certain biases or viewpoints.

- *Power dynamics.* Data is wielded by various entities – including governments, corporations and institutions – to make decisions and shape narratives. The control and manipulation of data can influence public opinion, policies and resource allocation, thus manifesting power dynamics.

- *Social implications.* The use and interpretation of data can impact different societal groups in different ways. For instance, healthcare data analysis might affect marginalized communities differently due to historical biases embedded in the data.

- *Agendas and influence.* Data can be used to advance specific agendas or ideologies. It is often employed strategically to influence perceptions, behaviours and even political outcomes, as seen in targeted advertising or political campaigning.

Essentially, this political perspective implies that data is not merely neutral information but rather a product of social, cultural and political contexts.[35] Acknowledging the political nature of data is important for digital leaders and decision makers. It ensures that they adopt a critical lens when analysing its origins, biases and implications, fostering a more nuanced understanding of the power dynamics inherent in its collection, interpretation and application.

The invisible hand of AI

These insights into data are particularly important as AI becomes widely adopted at every level within organizations. Companies and governments are increasingly turning to AI-powered tools to influence and predict human behaviour. Are digital leaders placing their organizations at risk if they do not have a deeper appreciation of the politics of AI?

There is no doubt about AI's power to influence behaviour in multiple spheres. From tailored political campaigns leveraging psychological profiling to sway elections[36] to platforms algorithmically nudging user engagement to encourage longer screen time,[37] the ethical boundaries of behaviour manipulation are being tested. Much of AI's influence can be considered benign, but it can also be argued that AI is subtly limiting our choices and shaping our perceptions of the world around us.

This manipulation, often invisible and subtle, has raised profound ethical questions about individual autonomy, freedom of information, and the potential for mass surveillance.[38] Case studies with troubling impacts abound. For example, in healthcare, algorithms trained on biased data can lead to discriminatory decisions about insurance coverage or treatment eligibility.[39] In advertising, targeted campaigns based on personal data can sway consumer choices and exploit vulnerabilities.[40]And in elections, the weaponization of data has been used to spread misinformation and manipulate voter behaviour.[41]

The importance of these themes is discussed in detail in Josh Simons's recent book *Algorithms for the People: Democracy in the Age of AI*.[42] Simons contends that the very act of prediction is infused with politics. From the design of predictive tools through to their implementation, human choices inevitably shape their impact. Through this political lens, Simons reimagines how democracies should govern decisions made outside traditional political channels, particularly those concerning predictive technologies.

Unsurprisingly, Simons sees a clear link between regulating these technologies and democratically reforming governance. Therefore, he argues, all those involved in the future of AI need to recognize the technology's political nature. This requires abandoning the limitations of conventional AI ethics discussions. Leaders must engage with deeper profound moral and political questions. Only then can we ensure that technology governance strengthens, rather than undermines, the very foundations of democracy.

One of the most important topics in Simons's book is the urgent need for leaders to ensure transparency and accountability in data governance, and this topic is receiving a great deal of attention as the world comes to grips with the impact of AI.[43] Simons's work highlights the importance of ensuring that data is collected ethically, used responsibly and protected from malicious actors. As he concludes, this requires robust regulations, public awareness campaigns and industry-wide collaboration to establish best practices for data management.

The road to responsible AI leadership

Building on Simons's ideas, we must recognize that the political impact of AI cannot be ignored. As leaders in the digital space, we have a duty to shape the future of AI responsibly. This results in three key messages for digital leaders.

1. *Manage data responsibly.* Recognize the inherent power and bias within data. Implement robust data governance frameworks that ensure transparency, accountability and fairness in data collection, usage and storage.

2. *Support ethical AI development.* Prioritize ethical considerations throughout the AI development lifecycle. Foster a culture of critical thinking and awareness of potential biases and unintended consequences.

3. *Encourage human-centred AI.* Remember that AI is a tool, not a replacement for human judgment and empathy. Strive to develop AI solutions that empower individuals, enable informed decision making and prioritize social good.

The politics of AI are complex and ever-evolving. As digital leaders, we have a responsibility to navigate this landscape with awareness, with responsibility and with a commitment to ethical AI development. By recognizing the power and potential pitfalls of AI, we can ensure that this transformative technology serves as a force for good, empowering individuals, shaping a more just future and tackling the critical challenges of our time.

Where to now?

The leadership challenges in digital transformation are not easily resolved. The key dilemma organizations face is whether to shape their leadership approach around well-understood leadership models that emphasize coordinated top-down decision making, or to seek substantially revised approaches towards less familiar techniques based on principles such as meritocracy and adhocracy.

There is no standard roadmap for resolving this dilemma. Each organization and individual must deal with it for themselves, in their own context, to address several important questions. For example, what is the leader's role in a decentralized, disrupted, data-driven world? How should leaders think and act to drive agile change in their organizations? How must existing leaders adapt to move from bureaucratic leadership to more of a meritocracy?

Of one thing there is no doubt: bringing a greater focus on these leadership questions will help AI adoption and accelerate digital transformation.

Key questions and next steps

How can organization leaders balance innovation and experimentation with the need for coordinated strategy and governance?

Initiate a culture that fosters innovation while maintaining strategic alignment and governance. Encouraging experimentation can be achieved through dedicated forums, such as innovation labs or cross-functional teams, where diverse perspectives converge to explore new ideas. Leaders must emphasize the importance of learning from failures and iterate quickly. Concurrently, establishing clear strategic frameworks and governance mechanisms ensures that experimentation aligns with broader organizational goals. Regular communication and collaboration channels should be established to share insights, align teams and maintain a coordinated approach across the organization.

How can leadership adapt to drive meaningful, sustained organizational change appropriate to the disruptive forces of AI?

To adapt to the fast-paced digital transformation journey, embrace agile management principles. This involves decentralizing decision-making processes, fostering rapid innovation cycles and encouraging a mindset of continuous learning. Digital leaders should invest in leadership development programmes that focus on agility, adaptability and collaboration. Creating interdisciplinary teams, leveraging short sprints and promoting the development of minimum viable products can accelerate the pace of change. Leaders should lead by example, showcasing agility in their decision making and adapting to emerging trends in the digital space.

What leadership traits are essential in navigating the complexities of a data-driven world typical of AI, and how can leaders transition from traditional models to embrace new approaches like adhocracy?

Leadership in a data-driven world requires a shift from traditional hierarchical models to more dynamic approaches. Invest in developing data literacy across your organization, ensuring that decision makers can leverage data effectively. Embracing meritocracy involves recognizing and rewarding expertise based on data-driven insights. For situations characterized by uncertainty and rapid change, leaders should explore adhocracy, promoting a culture of experimental learning and opportunistic risk taking. Customized leadership development programmes should guide leaders in transitioning from bureaucratic models to more agile, meritocratic and adhocratic approaches.

Further reading

Birkinshaw, Julian, and Jonas Ridderstrale. 2017. *Fast/Forward: Make Your Company Fit for the Future*. Stanford Business Books.

Ganesan, Kavita. 2022. *The Business Case for AI: A Leader's Guide to AI Strategies, Best Practices & Real-World Applications*. Opinosis Analytics Publishing.

Iansiti, Marco, and Karim Lakhani. 2020. *Competing in the Age of AI: Strategy and Leadership when Algorithms and Networks Run the World*. Harvard Business Review Press.

PART V

LOOKING INTO THE FUTURE OF AI

CHAPTER 13

The digital dilemmas that define AI's future

As leaders look to adopt AI, they must ask new questions and face complex ethical dilemmas. These include concerns about privacy, bias, job displacement and the need for control and transparency in AI development. An underlying issue in all of these is building trust in AI through responsible development and public discourse.

Major advances in AI dominate the headlines as individuals and organizations across the public and private sectors flock to the latest wave of generative AI solutions in record numbers. As a result, extensive investment in and experimentation with generative AI tools is taking place in almost every part of the economy[1] – and even more is planned for the coming year.[2]

While this progress is exciting, it has also sparked a growing sense of unease.[3] Indeed, the greatest impact of the recent wave of AI technology may not be the deployment of AI itself but the wakeup call it has provided as we face important questions about our digital future. Now more than ever, the digital world stands at a crossroads. As expectations surrounding AI's impact grow, so too do calls for a greater focus on its responsible development and use.[4] It is far from clear which path we should take, and the implications of the choices we make are also unknown. Leaders and decision makers looking to guide their organizations in the use of AI must now find ways to navigate this uncertain terrain. With so many emerging technologies, differences of perspective and competing objectives to address, there is no guidebook to follow. Instead, they must develop a deeper understanding of the disruptive impacts of AI by considering a series of critical dilemmas that are shaping our digital future.

Dilemma #1: privacy versus progress

The insatiable appetite of AI algorithms for data[5] fuels innovation, but it also raises concerns about how that data is gathered, managed, tagged and used. Facial recognition, social media tracking and even smart home devices generate mountains of personal data, often with murky consent or transparency.[6] This dilemma pits the convenience and benefits of AI against the fundamental right to privacy. Can we find a balance, or are we destined to trade one for the other?

This challenge is currently seen most clearly when we look at public sector organizations deploying AI-powered smart infrastructure in areas such as policing,[7] health monitoring[8] and traffic management.[9] Examples that are becoming more common include the use of facial recognition cameras to identify suspects in crowded spaces, CCTV for monitoring traffic flow by optimizing routes and reducing congestion, and smart sensors in buildings and homes for detecting air pollution and looking for defects. These advances undeniably improve our daily lives, but at what cost?

Constant surveillance raises a variety of concerns about privacy intrusion.[10] Who owns the data collected by these systems? How is it used? Can it be accessed by unauthorized individuals or organizations? The nebulous nature of consent further complicates the issue.[11] Are citizens and residents truly aware of the extent to which their data is being collected and used, or are they simply opting into convenience without fully understanding the implications? Broad surveys conducted in 2023 indicate that there is a great deal of scepticism about AI-powered data collection and widespread concern about how such data is secured, managed, traded and used.[12]

The dilemma becomes even more apparent when considering personal health data.[13] AI algorithms trained on medical records can predict disease outbreaks, personalize treatment plans and even identify individuals at risk for developing certain conditions. This has the potential to revolutionize healthcare at a time when cost efficiencies and quality improvements are essential to relieve pressure on both healthcare systems and professionals.[14] But it also raises concerns about data security and potential discrimination.[15] Imagine a scenario in which an individual's genetic data is used by an insurance company to deny coverage;[16] or consider an employer using information about perceived health risks to make hiring decisions[17]. These are the kinds of issues being faced today.

The challenge lies in finding a balance between the undeniable benefits of AI and the fundamental right to privacy. As we see in emerging AI regulations,[18] this is leading to a multi-pronged approach in which AI is developed and used within a well-defined governance framework. Issues in this area include the following.

- *Transparency and accountability.* Individuals need to be clearly informed about how their data is collected, used and stored. Organizations employing AI should be held accountable for data breaches and misuse.

- *Data protection laws.* Governments must enact and enforce robust data protection laws that give individuals control over their personal information.

- *Technological solutions.* Developers should prioritize privacy-preserving technologies – such as anonymization and differential privacy – that allow AI to function without compromising individual data.

- *Public education and awareness.* Raising public awareness about the implications of AI and data collection is crucial to fostering informed consent and encouraging responsible use of technology.

However, recent experiences have highlighted that the 'privacy versus progress' dilemma should not be oversimplified.[19] It is a tightrope walk, demanding constant vigilance and a commitment to finding solutions that protect individual rights while allowing AI to flourish. The hope is that by encouraging active engagement in this conversation and implementing robust safeguards, we can ensure that the benefits of AI are shared equitably and responsibly, without sacrificing the fundamental right to privacy that underpins a free and democratic society.

Dilemma #2: automation versus employment

AI-powered automation has been transforming industries for many years, replacing manual tasks with algorithms and robots.[20] While this promises increased efficiency and productivity, as the impact of AI on jobs broadens out to affect many more areas of the economy, fears are being raised[21] that it threatens widespread unemployment across many areas of professional services.[22] How can we ensure that the benefits of automation are shared equitably and that displaced workers are equipped with the skills to thrive in the new digital economy?

This dilemma – the tension between automation and employment – has been highly visible recently. Consider, for example, the case of the trucking industry. Self-driving trucks, touted for their safety and fuel efficiency, could potentially replace millions of truck drivers.[23] While this promises cost savings and safer roads, the potential human cost could be staggering.[24] The livelihood of countless families, many of which are already struggling in an increasingly competitive economy, may be badly affected. How can we ensure that the benefits of automation are shared equitably? Can we navigate this path without leaving a trail of unemployment and economic hardship?

One crucial approach to addressing this dilemma lies in reskilling and upskilling the workforce.[25] By investing in training programmes that equip displaced workers with the skills they need, the victims of automation can become its beneficiaries. This could include training in data analysis, robotics, cybersecurity and other fields poised for growth in the coming years. Finding, building and retaining the right digital skills is a major focus.[26]

Another potential solution is the concept of universal basic income.[27] This approach, which has been receiving renewed attention,[28] provides a guaranteed minimum income to every citizen, regardless of employment status, and it could offer a safety net for those displaced by automation while stimulating the economy through increased consumer spending. Recent comments by several prominent digital players, including Elon Musk,[29] have brought additional focus to this debate, galvanizing those on both sides of the argument.

Ultimately, addressing the automation versus employment dilemma requires collaborative effort. Businesses, governments, educational institutions and individuals must work together to ensure a smooth transition into the future of work.[30] A great deal of attention is focused on how to ensure a future in which automation does not create a chasm between the haves and have-nots, but instead sees its benefits being shared by all.[31]

Yet, managing the path forward for AI automation is not without its challenges. Implementing effective reskilling programmes, navigating the political complexities of wealth distribution, and ensuring responsible AI development are all daunting tasks. The potential rewards – a future in which auto-mation empowers rather than disenfranchises – are too great to ignore. One significant recent event was the AI safety summit at Bletchley Park in 2023.[32] This brought together a worldwide community to consider ways forward, and it raised hope that by embracing a spirit of collaboration and innovation we can ensure that the age of AI becomes not a time of fear and uncer-tainty, but a time of shared prosperity and progress.

Dilemma #3: bias versus fairness

AI algorithms are not immune to human biases.[33] When they are trained on data that is susceptible to human prejudice, they can perpetuate discrimination or even amplify it.[34] We have seen how this dilemma manifests in everything from biased hiring practices[35] to unfair loan approvals.[36] How can we ensure that AI is used ethically and responsibly, promoting fairness and inclusivity in a world increasingly shaped by algorithms?

The promise of AI lies in its ability to analyse vast amounts of data, leading to objective and efficient decisions, but this promise is tarnished by a hidden flaw: bias. Consider a financial institution using AI trained on historical data to decide on loans. While this data-driven decision making undoubtedly enhances efficiency, it has been found that using data derived from a vari-ety of historical activities might reflect systemic biases in access to credit,[37] disproportionately favouring certain demographics over others.[38] As a result, the algorithms used might systemat-ically deny loans to individuals from marginalized communities, even if they qualify financially.

Over the past year, institutions around the world have been highlighting the need to address algorithmic bias to ensure that AI is used ethically and responsibly, promoting fairness and inclusivity in a world increasingly governed by algorithms.[39] This starts with scrutinizing the data used to train AI models[40] to identify and mitigate potential biases by diversifying datasets, removing discriminatory features and employing techniques like fairness-aware data augmentation.[41] Also, key to progress are AI decision-making processes that are more transparent and understandable.[42] This allows for identifying and addressing biases within the algorithms themselves, ensuring that they are not operating without appropriate accountability. One approach is to implement mechanisms for human oversight of AI systems, ensuring that algorithmic decisions are ultimately subject to human review and ethical considerations.[43] This is crucial both to prevent discriminatory outcomes and to hold developers and users accountable for their actions.

A contributing factor to bias in AI systems is the lack of diversity in the teams responsible for AI development.[44] Fostering diversity and inclusion in AI development is an important focus.[45] Better system will be created if we encourage diverse teams of engineers, data scientists and ethicists to develop and deploy AI. This can help to identify and address biases from various perspectives, leading to fairer and more inclusive outcomes.

However, addressing bias in AI is not a one-time fix. It requires continuous vigilance, ongoing research and a commitment to ethical development and deployment. Leaders must constantly interrogate the data in use, the algorithms designed and the systems being built to ensure that they serve as tools for progress, not instruments of discrimination. By prioritizing fairness and inclusivity, AI can become a force for good, empowering individuals and building a more just and equitable society.

Dilemma #4: control versus autonomy

Fundamental to AI is its ability to evolve autonomously as it adapts to its operating context and learns about its environment. As AI becomes more sophisticated and is deployed more widely, the question of how it should be controlled has become increasingly pressing. Who is ultimately responsible for the decisions made by AI systems? Who pulls the plug when things go wrong? This dilemma raises profound questions about the future of human agency and the limits of AI autonomy in a world increasingly governed by machines.[46] It has even led some experts to call for a pause in AI development to allow time for reflection on how to find the right balance between these concerns.[47]

In practice, however, the pressure to keep moving forward seems overpowering. Consider, for example, the use of AI in the defence sector. Military conflicts such as those in Ukraine and Gaza have highlighted for many people the critical concerns we face as AI becomes more autonomous in decision making.[48] The Ukraine conflict has even been described as 'a living lab for AI warfare'.[49]

Perhaps the most visible example here is the use of military drones equipped with AI systems capable of identifying and targeting enemies.[50] Many aspects of their use are widely debated.[51] In the heat of battle, if the algorithm makes a fatal decision, misidentifying civilians as combatants, who is to blame? The programmer who coded the algorithm? The commander who deployed the drone? Or the AI itself, operating with effective autonomy? Such scenarios highlight the challenges of autonomous machines making life-or-death decisions, potentially beyond human control and accountability.[52]

Addressing this intricate maze of control and autonomy requires a careful balance to be struck. For many, maintaining a human-in-the-loop of decision making is essential to ensure human oversight for critical decisions, with AI acting as an advisor or decision-support tool.[53] This could involve requiring human authorization before autonomous systems take actions with significant consequences. But where do we draw the line between AI assistance and AI automation?

One approach is to focus on the transparency and explainability of AI decisions.[54] Demystifying AI algorithms requires making their decision-making processes transparent and understandable to all. This allows for human intervention when the logic behind an AI decision appears biased or flawed. The extent to which this is possible with the current complexity of AI algorithms is widely debated.[55]

Yet, at the heart of a controlled approach to AI is a strong ethical governance framework.[56] We have seen several organizations working to establish a robust ethical framework for AI development and deployment, emphasizing principles such as accountability, fairness and human oversight.[57] These frameworks can guide developers and policymakers in navigating the complex implications of algorithmic control. Recently released frameworks such as the US National Institute of Standards and Technology AI risk management framework are useful examples of the way forward.[58]

More broadly, current AI regulation efforts in both Europe[59] and the United States are looking to find the ideal scenario: one where they avoid stifling AI advancement with excessive control and find a sweet spot where autonomy fuels progress while remaining true to ethical principles and human accountability. As might be expected, different countries are taking different approaches. Recently released guidelines include a consolidation of China's rules on AI deployment;[60] President Biden's executive order on the 'Safe, Secure and Trustworthy Development and Use of AI';[61] and the UK government's white paper on its plans for AI regulation.[62]

Whether these strike the right balance between control and autonomy remains to be seen, and they can only be assessed within their specific cultural and political contexts. Regardless, adoption of these guidelines will require open dialogue; collaboration between technologists, policymakers and the public; and a constant vigil against the potential misuse of autonomous AI. Ultimately, the relationship between human control and AI autonomy will remain a complex and evolving issue. Leaders will be required to continuously adapt and refine their approaches as AI capabilities advance. This will be seen in emerging legal and regulatory frameworks, redefining the boundaries of human responsibility and fostering a culture of ethical AI development.

The failing: a lack of trust

In facing these dilemmas, a common thread emerges: a disturbing lack of trust in AI.[63] Surveys confirm that many people distrust the algorithms that shape our lives,[64] the companies that collect our data[65] and the governments that regulate those companies.[66] This failure of trust jeopardizes the foundation of a healthy digital society. Without trust, collaboration and open dialogue, we risk creating a future in which AI technology alienates rather than empowers.

Unfortunately, recent evidence shows that the lack of trust in AI is growing.[67] Across the algorithms that curate our newsfeeds, the companies that collect personal data and the government agencies tasked with ensuring responsible technological development, open questions are being raised about whether we are on the right track.[68] This trust deficit is not just a minor inconvenience: it is a growing chasm threatening the very foundations of a healthy and equitable digital society.

One of the main reasons for an increasing lack of trust in AI is its growing role in generating misinformation and deep fakes,[69] and their increasing use in misleading individuals.[70] The use of AI to influence individuals and communities is receiving increased attention.[71] For example, with major elections in the United Kingdom and United States planned for 2024, concerns have been raised about the extent to which AI-driven influencing will play a part in the results.[72]

Broader concerns are also being raised about AI's influence on what people see and hear online[73] and about the provenance of that information.[74] Many fear that without trust in information sources, informed discourse and collaborative problem solving become practically impossible. For example, when individuals scroll through social media feeds, rather than seeing a balanced mix of viewpoints on a controversial issue they see a curated stream of information based on their previous online viewing habits. While such personalization of content to an individual's preferences can be efficient, it also reduces choice and serves to confirm their existing biases. Additionally, this narrowing of choice is open to manipulation by AI algorithms, restricting access to particular information sources. Where this has been seen, it has caused a deepening of societal divides and eroded faith in fact-gathering approaches.[75]

Such data manipulation and the wider deployment of AI have broad geopolitical implications.[76] As the deep impact of AI grows, the political considerations of China, Europe and the United States have become more evident in the role that their governments play in AI's development. Not only is each of these state actors looking to manage access to AI capabilities within its own jurisdiction,[77] but a new form of 'AI cold war'[78] has also emerged in which access to the technologies that underpin AI are being restricted. This is having broad implications on how AI is being deployed across the world, and it is raising concerns about the way in which the technology is used or manipulated to support the state.

As a result, a key question facing us today is how we bridge this chasm and rebuild trust in the digital age. A starting point for many organizations and governments is to commit to transparent data practices, clearly outlining how information is collected, used and protected. This includes regular audits, accessible privacy policies and clear avenues for redress for data breaches. As we have seen in recent discussion about generative AI tools,[79] there are circumstances where it is far from clear how to resolve issues relating to provenance, ownership, copyright and intellectual property with some aspects of AI. Reaching agreement on such issues will be complex and difficult due to the wide variety of interests involved.

Giving individuals greater control over their data and online experiences is one possible approach to improved data management that has been receiving increased attention.[80] This could involve tools such as the Hub-of-All-Things,[81] which provides people with personal data stores, more granular privacy settings[82] and enhanced education on data use[83] to foster digital literacy. This includes support for use of ethical frameworks for AI development and deployment, prioritizing fairness, non-discrimination and human oversight.

Perhaps the most essential step, however, is fostering open and informed public discourse about the implications of AI technology on society.[84] This includes engaging diverse voices, actively listening to concerns and collaborating with civil society, academics and technologists to develop responsible solutions. In this way, rebuilding trust in the age of AI will become a shared responsibility demanding commitment from everyone – individuals, companies, policymakers and technologists. This is seen in increasing calls for a more informed public discourse on how we prioritize transparency, accountability and ethical development, ensuring that technology is seen to be an empowering force rather than an alienating one, fostering a future in which trust fuels progress and innovation benefits all of us.[85] This will remain a focus for many years to come.

Looking forward

There is no doubt that AI has gained a foothold in all our lives. With significant investment in recent years, generative AI advances have dominated recent headlines, encouraging organizations to experiment with its potential. Much has been achieved to bring increasing intelligence to core processes and to improve data-driven decision making. However, while this widespread investment in AI has pushed many organizations in the public and private sectors forwards in their digital transformation efforts, it has also forced leaders and decision makers to face up to a series of fundamental dilemmas.

As AI-driven systems have gathered more data, privacy concerns have increasingly collided with progress. Surveillance and data ownership have become central issues, prompting calls for transparency, stronger data-protection laws, privacy-enhancing technologies and increased public awareness. Balancing AI's benefits with individual rights has become a crucial challenge.

Meanwhile, fears about automation replacing jobs have sparked discussions about upskilling, and concepts such as universal basic income have reappeared on the agenda. These concerns are further amplified by exposed biases within AI algorithms, raising questions about fairness and ethical assessment. The tension between human control and AI autonomy underscores the need for transparent decision making and robust ethical governance.

Confronting these dilemmas has exposed a fundamental flaw: a lack of trust in AI, data practices and governance. Perhaps the most important recent lesson for leaders and decision makers is that rebuilding trust requires transparency, individual control over data, digital literacy and open dialogue among diverse stakeholders. This is essential for ensuring responsible technological development and a balanced, equitable digital future.

Key questions and next steps

How can organizations strike a balance between leveraging AI for innovation and respecting individuals' right to privacy?

Implement a well-defined governance framework involving transparency, accountability, stronger data-protection laws and privacy-preserving technologies. Ensuring individuals are informed about data collection, holding organizations accountable for misuse and promoting responsible AI development will be crucial. Public education and awareness campaigns can help in fostering informed consent and responsible use of technology.

How can the benefits of AI-powered automation be shared equitably, and what measures can be taken to equip displaced workers with the skills needed for the digital economy?

Focus on investing in reskilling and upskilling programmes to empower displaced workers with the skills required in the digital economy. Exploring concepts such as universal basic income can provide a safety net for those affected by automation, stimulating economic growth. Collaboration among businesses, governments, educational institutions and individuals is essential to ensure a smooth transition into the future of work.

How can AI be developed and deployed ethically to prevent biases and promote fairness and inclusivity?

Digital leaders can address this by scrutinizing and diversifying the datasets used to train their AI models. Implementing transparency and explainability in AI decision-making processes allows for human oversight. Fostering diversity in AI development teams ensures a range of perspectives to identify and mitigate biases. Continuous vigilance, research and a commitment to ethical AI development are necessary to prioritize fairness and inclusivity.

Further reading

Gowdat, Mo. 2022. *Scary Smart: The Future of Artificial Intelligence and How You Can Save Our World*. Bluebird.

Miller, Chris. 2023. *Chip War: The Fight for the World's Most Critical Technology*. Simon & Schuster.

Tegmark, Max. 2018. *Life 3.0: Being Human in the Age of Artificial Intelligence*. Penguin.

CHAPTER 14

Preparing for the next AI wave

AI hype is reaching fever pitch, but is it a bubble? Yes, undoubtedly, but it will still bring significant value for many organizations. Leaders should focus on delivering practical applications, addressing ethical considerations and building strong collaborative partnerships to navigate the hype and achieve sustainable results.

The last few years have witnessed a meteoric rise in the development and adoption of AI, and this has inevitably been mirrored by the hype surrounding it. From self-driving cars to automated customer service bots, AI has captured the imagination of the public and industry leaders alike. However, amidst this frenzy, concerns about an AI bubble loom large.[1] Similarities with the dot com bubble of the 1990s are being highlighted,[2] and there are even comparisons being made with the Dutch tulip bulb bubble in the 1600s.[3]

No surprise, then, that this is prompting questions about inflated expectations and the reality of achieving the potential of this transformative technology. Digital leaders navigating this dynamic landscape must address these concerns by adopting a critical yet optimistic lens to understand AI's true value proposition and to overcome its challenges. Are we experiencing an AI bubble? Yes, undoubtedly. But perhaps what matters now is learning how to make the most of this time of change, and planning how to exploit what is left when the bubble pops.

Hype versus reality: deconstructing the AI bubble

Despite its many exciting characteristics, AI is not a magic wand. While its potential is undeniable, the current narrative too often paints an unrealistic picture of its capabilities. Exaggerated claims about superhuman intelligence[4] and imminent robot takeovers[5] fuel a dangerous hype machine. This hype, and the inflated expectations it leads to, can lead to disappointment and disillusionment when the reality of AI's limitations and current state of development becomes apparent.[6]

Such challenges are most clearly seen when viewed from the perspective of large-scale adoption of AI in real-world scenarios,[7] particularly in legacy-laden areas of the public and private sectors. Here, a number of significant issues must be overcome.

- *Data challenges.* Access to clean, reliable and properly labelled data is crucial for effective AI implementation. Legacy systems often lack this infrastructure, hindering the development and deployment of robust AI solutions.

- *Talent and expertise.* Building and maintaining AI systems requires specialized skills and expertise in data science, machine learning and domain knowledge. The talent gap in these areas presents a significant hurdle.

- *Integration and interoperability.* Integrating AI solutions with existing systems and workflows can be complex and time consuming, especially in large organizations with diverse IT infrastructures.

- *Ethical considerations.* Concerns about bias, fairness and transparency in AI algorithms are paramount. Addressing these concerns through responsible development and deployment practices is crucial.

- *Regulatory uncertainty.* The evolving regulatory landscape surrounding AI adds another layer of complexity for businesses seeking to adopt this technology.

All of these issues, and others, reveal significant concerns about delivering digital change of any kind. With the escalating expectations surrounding AI, the tensions become much more intense as the gap between aspirations and reality grows.

A focus on what is left behind: the positive ripple effects of AI

In an insightful article written by Cory Doctorow at the end of 2023, the issue of what it means to be experiencing an AI bubble is directly addressed.[8] In addition to emphasizing its negative aspects, Doctorow argues that the aftermath of such bubbles can yield significant value. For example, he explains how WorldCom's fibreoptic bubble left us with important digital data capacity and usable infrastructure essential to delivering the benefits of cloud computing. He urges leaders and decision makers to look at the AI bubble in a similar light.

From his perspective, the AI bubble, characterized by massive investment, has led to a temporary surge in user satisfaction, fostering widescale experimentation and building productive communities around AI tools. However, he questions the sustainability of this model, highlighting the exorbitant costs associated with creating and maintaining large AI models. He raises concerns about the financial viability of currently proposed uses of AI. AI's main business model is focused on productivity gains and cost reduction. It faces challenges when the current AI usage model demands expensive human oversight due to AI's tendency to generate inaccurate results.

Consequently, he predicts a shrinking market for AI applications, particularly in high-profile safety-critical projects where costlier AI (requiring substantial human oversight) may not find widespread acceptance. Similarly, he sees equal challenges with attempts to succeed when applying AI in low-value, high-cost applications, expressing scepticism about their viability. Furthermore, compliance with increasingly stringent AI regulation will necessarily increase costs and reduce AI's immediate industry impact.

As a result, he urges us to look outside the AI bubble. For example, he predicts the survival of smaller AI models such as Hugging Face[9] and Llama,[10] which operate on commodity hardware. He also highlights the potential for federated learning and the proliferation of individuals skilled in statistical analysis and AI frameworks like PyTorch[11] and TensorFlow.[12] All of these he sees as positive outcomes.

Doctorow's comments highlight the lack of discussion among digital leaders about how to ride this wave to gain maximum value from the AI bubble. He questions the sustainability of current AI business models and advises cautious optimism about potential positive outcomes in terms of smaller models, federated learning and skill development in statistical analysis.

While Doctorow's warnings and advice are important in their own right, they also point to three broader considerations leaders should recognize as essential to surviving and thriving in the current AI bubble.

- *Acceleration of digital technology innovation.* The hype surrounding AI has spurred significant investment in research and development, leading to rapid advances in various related fields such as big data, machine learning and natural language processing. This has accelerated the overall pace of digital-technology innovation, benefiting many industries.

- *A change in attitude towards digital transformation.* The excitement surrounding AI has served as a wake-up call for many business leaders, highlighting the urgency of digital transformation. This shift in attitude is crucial for businesses to remain competitive in the digital age.

- *Renewed interest in planning for a fairer digital future.* Concerns about the potential societal impact of AI have led to a renewed focus on planning for a fairer and more equitable digital future. This includes discussions about responsible AI development, investment in digital skills training, and the need for appropriate regulatory frameworks.

When the bubble pops

For busy digital leaders and decision makers, navigating the AI hype and surviving the AI bubble requires a considered, balanced approach. Those making sustainable progress with AI adopt three main principles.

- *They focus on business value, not hype.* They do not get swept away by the hype. Instead, they focus on identifying specific business problems where AI can deliver tangible value and return on investment. To achieve this they start with small, achievable projects and scale gradually based on results.

- *They build the right foundation.* They address the fundamental challenges first. By investing in data infrastructure, talent development and ethical governance, they are able to ensure a smoother and more successful AI implementation.

- *They understand that collaboration is key.* They partner with experts, both internal and external, to bridge the knowledge gap and leverage the collective wisdom of their organization. Incentive models are adjusted to support collaborative behaviours and practices.

While the AI bubble will undoubtedly burst, the underlying advances in digital technology will continue to shape our future. The significance of AI lies beyond the hype. Leaders and decision makers must focus on practical considerations, address challenges and leverage the positive aspects of the AI phenomenon to steer their organizations towards a digitally transformed and ethically responsible future.

By focusing on real-world value, addressing challenges proactively and embracing collaboration, digital leaders can harness the power of AI to drive meaningful change and achieve their digital ambitions. Speeding up decision making and readjusting core business processes are essential steps that can be taken on the journey to AI adoption. By navigate the hype with a critical eye and adopting a pragmatic approach, leaders can focus on long-term value creation for their organization.

Key questions and next steps

How can digital leaders navigate the current AI bubble and distinguish between hype and reality?

Digital leaders should prioritize a critical evaluation of AI's true capabilities and limitations. Begin by conducting thorough research to understand the current state of AI development and its applicability to your industry. Consider key examples in your domain and others related to your context. Engage with experts and thought leaders to gain insights into realistic expectations. Establish internal guidelines for evaluating

AI solutions, emphasizing a focus on tangible business value rather than succumbing to exaggerated claims. Foster a culture of healthy scepticism within your organization to ask more informed questions, encouraging teams to critically assess the feasibility and benefits of AI implementations.

What are the key challenges hindering the large-scale adoption of AI, and how can they be effectively addressed?

To tackle these questions, digital leaders need to proactively address the challenges associated with AI implementation in real-world scenarios. Start by investing in robust data infrastructure to ensure access to clean and reliable data. Bridge the talent gap by fostering the development of skills in data science, machine learning and domain-specific knowledge. Streamline the integration of AI solutions with existing systems by adopting flexible and interoperable frameworks. Prioritize ethical considerations, implementing responsible development practices to address concerns about bias, fairness and transparency. Stay informed about the evolving regulatory landscape to navigate uncertainties effectively.

How can organizations leverage the positive ripple effects of the AI bubble and prepare for the post-bubble era?

Digital leaders must also strategize for the aftermath of the AI bubble. Experiment with smaller, open-source AI models such as Hugging Face and Llama, operating on commodity hardware. Embrace federated learning models and invest in developing individuals' skills in statistical analysis and popular AI frameworks such as PyTorch and TensorFlow. Encourage discussions and planning sessions within the organization to explore alternative AI business models that prioritize cost-effectiveness and sustainability. Position your organization to adapt to the changing market dynamics after the AI bubble has burst. This will ensure long-term viability and success.

Further reading

Simons, Josh. 2023. *Algorithms for the People: Democracy in the Age of AI*. Princeton University Press.

Yampolskiy, Roman. 2024. *AI: Unexplainable, Unpredictable, Uncontrollable*. Chapman & Hall.

CHAPTER 15

Delivering AI-at-Scale

As AI gains momentum, leaders will be responsible for delivering the benefits of AI across their organization: AI-at-Scale. This requires overcoming significant barriers to ensure AI's capabilities are widely adopted to support the organization's needs. How well this is carried out will determine AI's long-term success.

Widespread discussions about the opportunities and challenges of adopting AI broadly across large established organizations (LEOs) in the public and private sectors are driving high-level expectations about how fast and fundamental its effects will be.[1] Consequently, pressure is building to ensure that these ambitious goals for the return on investment in AI will be met. For example, statements from the UK government identify AI as being key to a major productivity boost that could automate up to 84% of repetitive service transactions[2] and lead to two-thirds of civil service jobs being replaced over the next fifteen years.[3]

Whether or not these ambitions will be realized remains to be seen. However, progress will depend on answering critical questions about how to scale AI adoption in practice. For example, what is the best way to convert lessons learned from experiments and pilot studies with AI into organization-wide change? What barriers must be overcome to introduce AI into established working practices? How can we turn early wins with AI into substantial measurable successes? And so on. These questions have many similarities with previous digital transformation experiences when moving to 'agile at scale' to deliver the benefits of flexible working practices across enterprises. Reviewing the lessons from these activities can inform the current wave of AI adoption needs as we seek to deliver AI-at-Scale.

Reviewing agile at scale experiences

Successfully deploying AI across a complex enterprise poses significant challenges. All forms of substantive change must face up to and overcome resistance. For LEOs pursuing highly disruptive digital changes, the barriers can be substantial. What can we learn from previous large-scale digital change efforts?

One of the most interesting avenues to explore is the way many organizations have adopted more agile ways of working. Particularly in areas of software and systems delivery, agile methods and approaches have gained a significant foothold over the past twenty years, but not without having to address many concerns about their scope, range, impact and applicability across diverse, complex environments. By examining the experiences of organizations that have adopted agile at scale, we can glean valuable insights that can be applied to navigating the potential pitfalls of large-scale AI adoption. An approach we can label AI-at-Scale.

Agile – a methodology emphasizing iterative development and rapid feedback loops – has become a cornerstone of modern software development.[4] While the core principles are well established, achieving 'agile at scale' presents a different hurdle. As with AI, scaling agile requires not just the adoption of certain practices but also the optimization of processes for collaboration across diverse stakeholder groups and the introduction of new ways of working into complex, legacy environments. While agile adoption often starts with enthusiastic developer teams, scaling these successes across an organization requires overcoming several key hurdles. Exploring these areas provides important insights for AI-at-Scale.

- *Resistance to change.* Traditional, plan-driven mindsets can clash with agile's emphasis on dynamic planning and rapid iteration. This creates a 'progressives versus traditionalists' divide, hindering widespread adoption. Misalignment of incentive models and project metrics creates tensions between agile aspirations and day-to-day controls.

- *Misaligned support teams.* Resource managers, financial teams and other supporting functions can struggle to adapt their practices to agile's less rigid planning and progress tracking. They may perceive it as disruptive to their established workflows aimed at maintaining consistency, lowering risk and minimizing deviations from existing plans.

- *Middle management challenges.* Project managers, analysts and those in other mid-level roles may feel threatened by the potential loss of control associated with empowered agile teams. Lack of understanding of agile team dynamics and progress creates a lack of trust across the different levels of an organization.

Examples of scaling agile: Bosch and USAA

In a 2018 review of attempts at scaling agile delivery, Darrel Rigby, Jeff Sutherland and Andy Noble reinforce these scaling issues and point to several important characteristics of successful agile adoption efforts in large organizations.[5] By exploring the experiences of several organizations, they identify three key levers that can be used to scale agile effectively.

First, they recommend that leaders responsible for agile delivery ensure that they are adopting agile practices themselves. Agile teams are self-organizing, with close customer connection, allowing faster innovation and freeing up senior leaders for strategic work. To lead agile transformations effectively, senior leaders should act as an agile team themselves, focusing on understanding customer needs and removing roadblocks.

Second, they observe that large companies must use a phased approach to implement the substantial changes required when adopting agile. Successful approaches to scaling start small, measure the impact and then decide whether to expand based on a cost–benefit analysis focused on value creation and organizational challenges. This allows for adjustments and avoids overwhelming changes.

Third, they highlight the importance of introducing agility widely across the organization. Creating isolated agile software delivery teams is just one element of scaling agile adoption. Successful agile organizations also focus on changing how these teams work with established structures to avoid slowdowns and ensure innovations are implemented effectively. This requires continuous adjustments in multiple areas throughout the organization, including functions such as project management, human resources, contracts management and procurement.

Two examples, drawn from their article, illustrate these concepts in practice. Bosch – a large global product and technology supplier with more than 400,000 employees and partners – initially struggled to implement agile when it employed a dual-organization approach in which some departments used agile practices while others stuck with more traditional approaches. This created conflict and hampered the overall transformation.

Greater progress was made once they expanded agile more broadly across the organization. Bosch later formed a steering committee with members from the board of management. This committee acted as an agile team itself, with members working collaboratively to remove roadblocks and solve problems. They also created a taxonomy to identify all the potential agile teams across the company. This experience highlights the importance of senior leadership buy-in and collaboration when adopting agile at scale. It emphasizes the dangers of implementing agile in a way that creates a two-tiered system within an organization.

A second example the authors describe is that of USAA: a large US-based banking and insurance organization providing services exclusively to military personnel, veterans and their families. In its approach to scaling agile, USAA organized its large workforce into a structure of several hundred agile teams. While at first glance this might seem overwhelming, taking this consistent approach across the whole organization helped them avoid confusion and disagreements by clearly defining the landscape of teams and their activities.

Then, when new projects were defined, project leaders could readily determine which team was responsible for each part of the customer experience, across all delivery channels (phone, website, app). This was especially important because USAA focuses on customer journeys that may cross several traditional departmental lines. The structure USAA defined connects agile teams to the people accountable for results, ensuring everyone is working together to deliver a seamless omnichannel experience providing value both to the organization and to the client.

Lessons learned from agile at scale for successful AI adoption

The experiences of adopting agile at scale offer valuable insights for organizations navigating the challenges of large-scale AI deployment. Both initiatives require not just implementing new technologies or practices, but also fostering a cultural shift that embraces structural reforms, leadership adaptation and substantial cross-departmental collaboration.

One of the key lessons that can be drawn is the importance of focusing scaling efforts on empowerment rather than disruption. As with concerns around agile replacing traditional project management roles, fears of AI displacing human workers can hinder adoption. By framing AI as a tool to enhance existing functions and by empowering stakeholders to understand its contribution, organizations foster a more positive and collaborative environment in which AI can flourish.

Another crucial lesson is the value of using a phased implementation approach when introducing substantive change. Just as agile adoption often started with successful pilot projects, AI initiatives should begin with targeted use cases that showcase the technology's value proposition. This allows for incremental scaling, continuous improvement and adaptation of existing workflows to address concerns and ensure a smooth integration of AI.

Building bridges between technical teams and supporting functions is another critical element seen in these examples. The challenges faced delivering agile at scale – where project planning experts, resource managers and finance teams struggled to adapt to agile's flexible delivery rhythm – mirror the hurdles now being experienced with largescale AI adoption. Fostering open communication and ensuring a clear understanding of how AI tools interact with existing processes and roles is essential for successful integration.

Hence, by applying the lessons learned from agile at scale, organizations can navigate the complexities of large-scale AI adoption more effectively. A focus on collaboration, empowerment and a phased approach can unlock the full potential of AI while minimizing disruption and maximizing the value it delivers to an organization.

Towards AI-at-Scale

However, bridging the gap from early pilot studies to large-scale adoption of AI solutions – what we broadly refer to as AI-at-Scale – faces challenges[6] familiar to anyone involved with digital transformation efforts over the past decade.[7] While small-scale experiments and limited use cases abound, expanding the range, application and resilience of those solutions is proving to be a much more difficult task.[8] Obtaining sufficient high-quality data, integrating AI with existing systems, overcoming talent shortage and managing ethical considerations are just a few of the many key hurdles faced by organizations as they take on this task.

Surveys, research and case studies of AI adoption all indicate that leaders must address these issues to unlock the true potential of AI and bring its benefits to all those in an organization.[9] But where should organizations place their focus? And how do digital leaders identify the priority barriers to be overcome to accelerate AI adoption?

To make progress, a critical first step is to define the challenges being faced in delivering AI-at-Scale by learning from those around us. To help in this task, we can examine the results of two major initiatives that shine a spotlight on the issues and provide lessons on how to accelerate AI-at-Scale. The first of these is a broad survey conducted by the Digital Leaders network[10] into the attitudes of digital leaders towards adoption and use of AI.[11] The second is a study carried out by the UK National Audit Office (NAO) that involved a more substantial examination of the current use of AI across UK government agencies.[12]

The Digital Leaders 'AI attitudes survey 2024'

At the end of 2023, an online survey of digital leaders' attitudes towards AI use in their organizations was conducted by the Digital Leaders community. It resulted in 577 completed responses, with the majority (50%) from the public sector and the remainder split between the private sector (28%), the charity sector (17%) and academia (5%). What makes this survey particularly valuable is the seniority of those responding: 58% of respondents identified themselves as digital leaders at C-suite level, with the remaining 42% being at the senior management team level.

The results of this survey confirm widespread interest in AI from all digital leaders, but they also highlight the challenges those leaders perceive in AI adoption, such as the need for better data management infrastructure, the high cost of talent acquisition and development, and the lack of robust ethical frameworks for successful adoption. Reviewing the detailed responses reveals five key points that offer a broad snapshot of the state of AI-at-Scale.

- *AI is already widely discussed.* AI is a major topic among digital leaders, with most survey respondents reporting weekly discussions and interactions with AI, and more than a third using it daily. This frequent engagement is driving significant debate about AI at senior leadership levels.

- *AI use is a mixed picture.* While awareness of AI is high, many of those surveyed have not identified practical uses for it or assessed its business impact. This lack of clear strategy extends to generative AI, with most organizations lacking policies to govern its use.

- *AI adoption is causing challenges.* Implementing AI faces hurdles common to previous digital transformation efforts in large organizations. While concerns about return on investment exist (with almost half of respondents being unsure of a positive impact), bigger issues lie in talent acquisition and retention and in integrating AI into existing workflows (both cited by over half as significant barriers). Interestingly, fears of job losses were a concern for fewer respondents (less than a quarter).

- *AI impact on systems performance is unclear.* Despite interest in AI, there are concerns about its real-world use. Reliability and data privacy are major issues, with less than a quarter of respondents having confidence in AI for critical tasks and more than 90% saying they were worried about data privacy.

- *AI brings new leadership concerns.* Digital leaders prioritize building trust in AI by tackling ethics, bias and transparency. However, the survey reveals a concerning lack of preparedness for upcoming regulations and responsible AI frameworks, with more than 60% of respondents expressing worries in these areas.

Overall, the Digital Leaders AI attitudes survey confirms the high expectations being created for AI in many organizations. However, it also reinforces concerns from leaders about their ability to scale AI adoption in a responsible and appropriate way.

The UK National Audit Office's 'AI in government' study

In contrast to the Digital Leaders survey's focus on AI attitudes, the March 2024 NAO report presents a more detailed and comprehensive review of the current state of AI adoption across the UK government. It is based on combining insights from a survey completed by eighty-nine government bodies, a selection of in-depth interviews, four case study descriptions and substantial background research. The report summarizing the study is a value for money assessment submitted to parliament to monitor ongoing actions on AI deployment and to provide input to future UK government policy actions.

Recent UK government statements have highlighted the potential of AI to transform public services in the United Kingdom,[13] emphasizing its importance in generating performance improvements and driving cost savings.[14] Based on these aspirations, the government has been developing strategies to leverage AI[15] and it is supporting its agencies to expand AI use through a number of investments and incentives.[16] In this context, the NAO value for money study was designed to understand approaches to AI use across the UK government to maximize the opportunities and mitigate the risks in delivering AI benefits in the provision of public services.

The key finding from the study was that while some government bodies have begun implementing AI, widespread adoption is in its early stages and remains limited. The report highlights that achieving AI-at-Scale requires not only technological investment, but also significant changes to internal practices, external governance processes and workforce capabilities. Historically, meeting these needs has been found to be severely challenging in large-scale digital change programmes in UK government.[17] The study therefore emphasizes that applying the lessons from these experiences will be important to meet expectations as the UK government drives its AI-at-Scale ambitions forward.

Additionally, the NAO study found that there are specific areas of concern to address if the UK government is to broaden its AI adoption and meet the targets being set for AI deployment. Among the most challenging barriers to address, as highlighted in its survey, is the need for further support to address potential legal risks, improve privacy and data protection, and defend against cyber attacks and security breaches.

Unsurprisingly given the context, the NAO study also placed a particular spotlight on the strength of the relationships that exist between the various UK government agencies that have responsibility for defining, delivering and assessing progress in AI adoption. As with any large, complex organization, the internal structures, processes and mechanisms for governance play an important role in determining the pace at which widescale change can be carried out. In particular, the report identifies the tensions that exist between government teams focused on driving AI innovation in specific domains and the risk avoidance culture that surrounds the range of compliance, reporting, assessment and governance obligations that are essential in public sector activities.

Achieving AI-at-Scale requires finding ways to balance these competing concerns by improving communication, encouraging knowledge and asset sharing, and clarifying overlapping roles and responsibilities.

In sustaining large-scale AI adoption activities, the NAO report highlights the importance of robust central support, including ensuring clear ownership of the AI strategy, aligning funding allocation efforts and refining implementation plans to emphasize measurable goals. Furthermore, the report emphasizes the importance of tying AI adoption to core digital transformation improvements including modernizing IT infrastructure, developing a skilled workforce and establishing clear guidelines for managing risks such as data bias and data security. By effectively addressing these considerations, the report suggests that the transformative potential of AI in public services can be brought more sharply into focus.

Taking the next steps in AI-at-Scale

Both of the studies discussed above draw attention to the barriers that must be addressed to meet the challenge of delivering AI-at-Scale. The combined insights from the Digital Leaders survey and the NAO study offer valuable lessons for all digital leaders looking to accelerate responsible and impactful AI-at-Scale adoption within their organizations. These can be summarized as follows.

- *Bridge the gap between ambition and action.* While interest in AI is high, organizations lack clear strategies for implementation and therefore struggle to meet expectations. Leaders must prioritize identifying practical use cases with a demonstrable return on investment, ensuring alignment with core business goals.

- *Prioritize talent and infrastructure.* Skilled talent and robust data infrastructure are fundamental for successful AI integration. Leaders must match ambitions to their investment in talent acquisition, development and reskilling programmes focused on expanding AI expertise. Additionally, a focus on modernizing IT infrastructure is essential to support the data ingestion, storage and analysis required for AI operations.

- *Build trust and mitigate risks.* Being explicit about ethical considerations and data privacy concerns is paramount. Leaders must prioritize developing robust governance frameworks for AI development and deployment. This includes establishing clear lines of authority, communicating guidelines for data management, addressing potential biases in algorithms, and ensuring responsible AI use is aligned with rapidly changing regulations.

By addressing these key lessons, digital leaders can accelerate the path towards AI-at-Scale, unlock the true potential of AI and enable their organizations to leverage this transformative technology responsibly and effectively.

Key questions and next steps

How can digital leaders prepare for the challenges of delivering AI-at-Scale?

To prepare, bridge the gap between ambition and action by prioritizing use cases with a clear return on investment that align with your business goals. Invest in talent and infrastructure by identifying skill gaps and upskilling your workforce, while simultaneously modernizing IT systems to handle AI's data demands. Build trust by establishing a clear ethical framework for AI development, and prioritize responsible use of the technology. By addressing these areas, you can create momentum towards unlocking the potential of AI-at-Scale.

How can we invest in talent development and IT modernization to ensure we have the necessary resources for AI-at-Scale?

Conduct a skills gap analysis to identify areas where AI expertise is needed. Invest in training programmes and reskilling initiatives to equip your workforce with the necessary AI knowledge and capabilities. Develop a plan to modernize IT infrastructure, focusing on the data storage, processing and analytics capabilities required for AI operations.

How can we build trust and mitigate risks associated with adopting AI-at-Scale?

Develop a comprehensive ethical framework for AI development and deployment that prioritizes responsible use of the technology. Establish clear lines of authority for AI projects and ensure effective communication of data management guidelines throughout the organization. Implement robust governance procedures to address potential biases in algorithms and ensure compliance with evolving regulations surrounding AI use. Proactively address privacy concerns by creating clear data protection policies and fostering transparency around how data is collected, stored and used.

Further reading

Denning, Steve. 2018. *The Age of Agile: How Smart Companies Are Transforming the Way Work Gets Done*. Amaryllis.

Lee, Kai-Fu, and Chen Qiufan. 2021. *AI 2041: Ten Visions for Our Future*. W. H. Allen.

Mollick, Ethan. 2024. *Co-Intelligence: Living and Working with AI*. W. H. Allen.

Acknowledgements

Writing a book is big undertaking, requiring a lot of work over a long period. It is only possible with a great deal of help and support. It is my pleasure to acknowledge the contributions that many people have made on this journey.

Many thanks to my friends and colleagues for their guidance, help and support in developing my understanding of these topics. I have learned so much from my discussions with you to challenge my thinking and broaden my perspective. Without you this book would not have been possible.

As always, there are too many people to thank to name everyone individually, but I would particularly like to acknowledge the impact that the insights of the following people has had on my work: Saeema Ahmed-Kristensen, Christine Ashton, Dave Birch, Nawtej Dosanjh, Tim Field, Jerry Fishenden, David Frohlich, Yvonne Gallagher, James Herbert, Jon Holt, David Knight, Robin Knowles, David Lopez, Roger Maull, Tony Moretta, Rashik Parmar, Bill Payne, Sacha Rook, Travis Street, Mark Thompson, Dave West, Leroy White and Zena Wood.

The ideas in this book have also benefited from various collaborative projects over the past few years: most notably the Defence Data Research Centre (DDRC), funded by the Defence Science and Technology Laboratory (Dstl); and the DIGIT Lab, funded by the UK Engineering and Physical Sciences Research Council (EPSRC).

My ideas have also benefited from the help and support of Robin Knowles, the founder of Digital Leaders, and this book directly addresses the concerns of that community of experts. Many thanks for all the valuable discussions and insights.

Given the topic and focus of the book, I would also like to acknowledge the use of a variety of AI tools in its creation and review. AI tools such as ChatGPT, Gemini, Claude and others have been an important aid and have been used to conduct topic *searches*, make improvement *suggestions*, create text *summaries*, and provide content *snippets* – what I refer to as the '4S approach'. Use of AI tools in this way has allowed me to focus on developing the narrative that runs throughout the book, deriving insights from a diverse set of sources and bringing together the key themes in the most effective way.

I would also like to thank Richard Baggaley and Sam Clark from London Publishing Partnership. Their hard work and experienced guidance have been exceptional in bringing this book together.

And most of all, a big thank you to my family for their endless love and support throughout the writing of this book, and always.

About the author

Alan is a professor in digital economy, an experienced business executive and a strategic advisor. He has spent more than thirty years in the United States, Europe and the United Kingdom driving large-scale software-driven programmes with commercial high-tech companies, leading R&D teams, building state-of-the-art solutions and improving software product delivery approaches.

Alan now engages in business consulting, advisory work and research with a variety of organizations across many sectors. Alan holds a professorship in digital economy at the University of Exeter, where he co-founded Exeter's initiative in the digital economy (INDEX) and plays a key role in the Defence Data Research Centre: a £4 million research programme funded by the Defence Science and Technology Lab that is investigating AI and data science in the defence sector. He is a fellow of the British Computer Society and recently completed his role as a fellow at the Alan Turing Institute, the UK's national institute for data science and AI.

Throughout his career, Alan has written a wide variety of books and papers on topics such as enterprise software engineering, systems design, agile delivery and digital business transformation. Alan's latest work explores the growing impact of AI on business and how to deploy AI-at-Scale. His focus is on helping leaders learn to survive and thrive in the age of AI.

Further details on this book's content can be found at www.SurviveAIBook.com. Alan's own personal website can be found at www.AlanBrown.net.

Notes

All links were validated on 12 March 2024.

Introduction

1 https://www.forbes.com/sites/forbestechcouncil/2023/11/09/
standing-on-the-brink-the-untold-impact-of-generative-ai-on-
society/?sh=f9d5eeb43299.
2 https://www.bloomberg.com/news/articles/2023-11-01/
ai-doomers-take-center-stage-at-the-uk-s-ai-summit.
3 https://www.economist.com/business/2023/11/19/
the-sam-altman-drama-points-to-a-deeper-split-in-the-tech-world.

Chapter 1

1 https://www.bcg.com/publications/2018/
not-digital-transformation-without-digital-culture.
2 Jordan, John M. 2017. Challenges to large-scale organization: the case
of Uber. *Journal of Organization Design* 6: 11 (https://link.springer.
com/content/pdf/10.1186/s41469-017-0021-2.pdf).
3 https://www2.deloitte.com/content/dam/Deloitte/us/Documents/
process-and-operations/us-the-two-speed-organization.pdf.
4 https://www.brynjolfsson.com/.
5 https://www.andrewmcafee.org/.
6 https://www.thomaslfriedman.com/.
7 https://en.wikipedia.org/wiki/Triple_bottom_line.
8 https://www.mckinsey.com/capabilities/
strategy-and-corporate-finance/our-insights/the-great-acceleration.
9 https://www2.deloitte.com/us/en/insights/topics/digital-
transformation/digital-transformation-survey.html.
10 https://www.forbes.com/sites/
chunkamui/2017/04/04/7-steps-for-inventing-the-future.
11 Mele, Nicco. 2014. *The End of Big: How the Internet Makes David the
New Goliath.* Picador.

12 https://www.weforum.org/agenda/2021/05/
    what-gig-economy-workers/.
13 Uludağ, O., P. Philipp, A. Putta, M. Paasivaara, C. Lassenius and
    F. Matthes. 2022. Revealing the state of the art of large-scale agile
    development research: a systematic mapping study. *Journal of
    Systems and Software* 194: article 111473 (https://www.sciencedirect.
    com/science/article/abs/pii/S0164121222001601).
14 https://en.wikipedia.org/wiki/Lean_startup.
15 Denning, Steven. 2010. *A Leader's Guide to Radical Management:
    Reinventing the Workplace for the 21st Century*. Jossy-Bass.
16 https://www.imd.org/reflections/servant-leadership.

Chapter 2

1   https://info.digital.ai/digital-transformation-progress-report.html.
2   https://www.kotterinc.com/8-steps-process-for-leading-change/.
3   https://www.mckinsey.com/business-functions/strategy-and-
    corporate-finance/our-insights/how-covid-19-has-pushed-companies-
    over-the-technology-tipping-point-and-transformed-business-forever.
4   https://news.microsoft.com/
    en-my/2020/05/04/2-years-of-digital-transformation-in-2-months/.
5   https://news.microsoft.com/2021/05/06/new-study-shows-digital-
    preparedness-helped-organizations-adapt-to-covid-19/.
6   https://www.cio.com/article/3234366/7-simple-ways-to-fail-at-agile.
    html.
7   https://enterprisersproject.com/article/2020/6/
    digital-transformation-how-keep-momentum.
8   https://www.computerweekly.com/news/252509159/
    HMRC-IT-transformation-plans-under-strain-says-NAO-report.
9   https://en.wikipedia.org/wiki/Technical_debt.
10 https://www.computerweekly.com/opinion/
    Digital-government-problems-on-the-horizon.
11 https://www.gartner.com/en/newsroom/press-releases/2023-07-27-
    gartner-survey-finds-55-of-organizations-that-have-deployed-ai-take-
    an-ai-first-strategy-with-new-use-cases.
12 https://www.forbes.com/sites/joemckendrick/2021/09/12/
    digital-transformation-is-only-the-beginning-a-companys-journey.
13 Schaffer, Robert H. 2017. All management is change management.
    Harvard Business Review, October (https://hbr.org/2017/10/
    all-management-is-change-management).
14 https://www.bmc.com/blogs/lewin-three-stage-model-change.

15 Brown, A.W. 2013. *Enterprise Software Delivery: Bringing Agility and Efficiency to the Global Software Supply Chain.* Pearson.
16 https://www.nao.org.uk/reports/digital-transformation-in-government.
17 https://en.wikipedia.org/wiki/John_Kotter.
18 https://www.kotterinc.com/methodology/8-steps.
19 Kotter, John. 2012. Accelerate! *Harvard Business Review,* November (https://www.kotterinc.com/wp-content/uploads/2017/06/OFFICIAL-_-Accelerate-HBR-Nov_2012_print-1.pdf).

Chapter 3

1 https://www.techrepublic.com/article/ibm-watson-the-inside-story-of-how-the-jeopardy-winning-supercomputer-was-born-and-what-it-wants-to-do-next/.
2 https://www.newscientist.com/article/2079871-im-in-shock-how-an-ai-beat-the-worlds-best-human-at-go/.
3 https://www.bcg.com/publications/2023/how-generative-ai-transforms-customer-service.
4 https://www.techradar.com/pro/uk-government-set-to-trial-ai-services-to-replace-civil-servants.
5 https://arxiv.org/abs/2304.02017.
6 https://www.techradar.com/news/the-ncsc-warns-of-the-dangers-of-chatgpt.
7 https://www.theguardian.com/technology/2023/mar/31/ai-research-pause-elon-musk-chatgpt.
8 https://www.fastcompany.com/90826178/generative-ai.
9 https://www.nytimes.com/2023/03/28/technology/ai-chatbots-chatgpt-bing-bard-llm.html.
10 https://hai.stanford.edu/news/how-large-language-models-will-transform-science-society-and-ai.
11 https://www.nature.com/articles/s42254-023-00581-4.
12 https://aimi.stanford.edu/events/can-chatgpt-diagnose-me-how-large-language-models-will-transform-clinical-care.
13 https://arxiv.org/abs/2212.13138.
14 https://www.llmstudy.com/blog/Why-it-is-the-perfect-time-to-study-an-LLM-in-Health-Care-Law.
15 https://www.thelancet.com/journals/lancet/article/PIIS0140-6736(23)00216-7.
16 https://www.forbes.com/sites/lutzfinger/2023/03/27/large-language-models--ai-in-healthcare.

17 https://www.mckinsey.com/capabilities/quantumblack/our-insights/
the-state-of-ai-in-2023-generative-AIs-breakout-year.

Chapter 4

1   https://www.eweek.com/cloud/
bill-gates-says-we-re-living-in-a-golden-age-of-computer-science.

2   https://cio.economictimes.indiatimes.com/news/cloud-
computing/why-2020-will-be-marked-as-the-golden-age-of-cloud-
computing/79912500.

3   Ng, Irene. 2014. *Creating New Markets in the Digital Economy: Value
and Worth*. Cambridge University Press.

4   https://www.gartner.com/en/newsroom/press-releases/2019-02-20-
gartner-survey-reveals-digital-twins-are-entering-mai.

5   Hennessy, John L., and David A. Patterson. 2019. A new golden age
for computer architecture. *Communications of the ACM* 62(2): 48–60
(https://dl.acm.org/doi/10.1145/3282307).

6   https://www.techradar.com/news/
what-is-ai-everything-you-need-to-know.

7   https://www.ibm.com/topics/neural-networks.

8   https://www.ibm.com/topics/deep-learning.

9   https://mitsloan.mit.edu/ideas-made-to-matter/
machine-learning-explained.

10 https://ai.google/discover/generativeai.

11 https://www.gsb.stanford.edu/insights/
andrew-ng-why-ai-new-electricity.

12 Friedman, Thomas. 2016. *Thank You for Being Late: An Optimist's Guide
to Thriving in the Age of Accelerations*. Farrar, Straus and Giroux.

13 https://theconversation.com/ai-can-book-a-restaurant-or-a-hair-
appointment-but-dont-expect-a-full-conversation-96720.

14 Crawford, Kate. 2021. *Atlas of AI: Power, Politics, and the Planetary
Costs of Artificial Intelligence*. Yale University Press.

15 https://www.forbes.com/sites/cognitiveworld/2019/09/17/
the-seven-patterns-of-ai.

16 https://www.mckinsey.com/industries/automotive-and-assembly/
our-insights/autonomous-drivings-future-convenient-and-connected.

17 https://arstechnica.com/cars/2023/09/
are-self-driving-cars-already-safer-than-human-drivers/.

18 https://www.forbes.com/sites/cognitiveworld/2019/07/26/
how-ai-can-transform-the-transportation-industry.

19 Agrawal, Ajay, Joshua Gans and Avi Goldfarb. 2022. *Prediction Machines: The Simple Economics of Artificial Intelligence.* Harvard Business Review Press.

20 https://www.forbes.com/sites/qai/2023/01/06/applications-of-artificial-intelligence.

21 https://www.mckinsey.com/capabilities/operations/our-insights/ai-driven-operations-forecasting-in-data-light-environments.

22 https://www.iea.org/commentaries/why-ai-and-energy-are-the-new-power-couple.

23 https://www.forbes.com/sites/forbesbusinesscouncil/2023/11/20/harnessing-ais-potential-to-revolutionize-financial-forecasting.

24 https://www.metoffice.gov.uk/about-us/press-office/news/corporate/2023/ai-to-take-weather-forecasting-by-storm.

25 https://www2.deloitte.com/uk/en/blog/experience-analytics/2021/state-of-ai-in-uk-healthcare-industry.html.

26 https://www.weforum.org/agenda/2021/07/ai-machine-learning-bias-discrimination.

27 https://kpmg.com/us/en/articles/2023/artificial-intelligence-survey-23.html.

28 https://www.jaronlanier.com/.

29 https://www.theguardian.com/technology/2023/mar/23/tech-guru-jaron-lanier-the-danger-isnt-that-ai-destroys-us-its-that-it-drives-us-insane.

30 https://www.theguardian.com/technology/2022/nov/27/jaron-lanier-tech-threat-humanity-twitter-social-media.

31 https://kozyrkov.medium.com/whats-different-about-today-s-ai-380569e3b0cd.

32 https://www.theguardian.com/commentisfree/2023/may/03/ai-chatgpt-bard-artificial-intelligence-apocalypse-global-rules.

33 https://en.wikipedia.org/wiki/AI_winter.

34 https://www.mckinsey.com/featured-insights/artificial-intelligence/the-promise-and-challenge-of-the-age-of-artificial-intelligence.

35 https://www.theguardian.com/technology/2023/feb/02/chatgpt-100-million-users-open-ai-fastest-growing-app.

36 https://kozyrkov.medium.com/.

37 https://www.tabletmag.com/sections/news/articles/oy-ai-jaron-lanier.

38 https://www.theguardian.com/technology/2021/jun/06/microsofts-kate-crawford-ai-is-neither-artificial-nor-intelligent.

39 https://www.theguardian.com/technology/2023/mar/23/tech-guru-jaron-lanier-the-danger-isnt-that-ai-destroys-us-its-that-it-drives-us-insane.

40 https://www.techradar.com/news/microsofts-new-data-dignity-team-aims-to-give-users-more-control-over-their-data.

41 Lanier, Jaron, and E. Glen Weyl. 2018. A blueprint for a better digital society. *Harvard Business Review*, September (https://hbr.org/2018/09/a-blueprint-for-a-better-digital-society).

42 https://theodi.org/insights/explainers/what-is-a-data-trust/.

43 Zuboff, Shoshana. 2019. *The Age of Surveillance Capitalism: The Fight for a Human Future at the New Frontier of Power*. Profile Books.

44 https://www.nytimes.com/2021/01/10/technology/tim-berners-lee-privacy-internet.html.

45 https://www.youtube.com/watch?v=J61ZV1si3V4.

46 https://medium.com/hub-of-all-things/personal-data-as-currency-ab1590163ad6.

47 https://www.theguardian.com/technology/2023/mar/23/tech-guru-jaron-lanier-the-danger-isnt-that-ai-destroys-us-its-that-it-drives-us-insane.

Chapter 5

1   Sommerville, Ian. 2017. *Software Engineering*, 10th edition. Pearson.

2   https://www.techopedia.com/definition/8982/procedural-language.

3   https://www.technipages.com/definition/declarative-programming-language.

4   https://www.amazon.com/Enterprise-Software-Delivery-Bringing-Efficiency/dp/0321803019.

5   https://en.wikipedia.org/wiki/AI_winter.

6   https://www.statista.com/statistics/607716/worldwide-artificial-intelligence-market-revenues.

7   https://www.techtarget.com/searchstorage/definition/terabyte.

8   https://setiathome.berkeley.edu/cpu_list.php.

9   https://www.python.org/.

10 https://github.com/.

11 https://www.tensorflow.org/.

12 https://www.techrepublic.com/topic/artificial-intelligence.

13 https://towardsdatascience.com/reading-list-for-applied-ai-5f4b84c75c1f.

14 https://towardsdatascience.com/the-complete-list-of-books-for-quantitative-algorithmic-machine-learning-trading-621b274fec5f.

15 https://www.forbes.com/sites/bernardmarr/2023/06/02/the-15-biggest-risks-of-artificial-intelligence.

16 https://www.weforum.org/agenda/2020/02/
where-is-artificial-intelligence-going.

17 https://digileaders.substack.com/p/
to-pause-or-to-push-on-the-ai-dilemma.

18 https://www.bloomberg.com/news/articles/2023-04-07/
former-google-ceo-rejects-ai-research-pause-over-china-fears.

19 https://en.wikipedia.org/wiki/Turing_test.

20 Hernandez-Orallo, Jose. 2020. Twenty years beyond the Turing Test:
moving beyond the human judges too. *Minds and Machines* 30: 533–
562 (https://link.springer.com/article/10.1007/s11023-020-09549-0).

21 https://en.wikipedia.org/wiki/Generative_artificial_intelligence.

22 https://en.wikipedia.org/wiki/Large_language_model.

23 https://www.techrepublic.com/article/ibm-watson-the-inside-story-
of-how-the-jeopardy-winning-supercomputer-was-born-and-what-it-
wants-to-do-next.

24 https://en.wikipedia.org/wiki/Deep_learning.

25 https://en.wikipedia.org/wiki/Neural_network.

26 https://futurism.com/
amazons-ceo-says-were-living-in-the-golden-age-of-ai.

27 https://www2.deloitte.com/us/en/pages/consulting/articles/the-
future-of-ai.html.

28 McKendrick, Joe, and Andy Thurai. 2022. AI isn't ready to make
unsupervised decisions. *Harvard Business Review*, September (https://
hbr.org/2022/09/ai-isnt-ready-to-make-unsupervised-decisions).

29 https://www.forbes.com/sites/ashleystahl/2022/05/03/
the-rise-of-artificial-intelligence-will-robots-actually-replace-people.

30 https://www.bloomberg.com/news/features/2022-10-06/
even-after-100-billion-self-driving-cars-are-going-nowhere.

31 https://www.theguardian.com/technology/2022/mar/27/
how-self-driving-cars-got-stuck-in-the-slow-lane.

32 https://towardsdatascience.
com/3-ways-leaders-fail-their-ai-projects-fcaf98e9bb8a.

33 Davenport, Thomas H., and Rajeev Ronanki. 2018. Artificial
intelligence for the real world. *Harvard Business Review*, February
(https://hbr.org/2018/01/artificial-intelligence-for-the-real-world).

Chapter 6

1 McKendrick, Joe. 2021. AI adoption skyrocketed over the last 18
months. *Harvard Business Review*, September (https://hbr.org/2021/09/
ai-adoption-skyrocketed-over-the-last-18-months).

2   https://www.theguardian.com/technology/2021/jun/06/
microsofts-kate-crawford-ai-is-neither-artificial-nor-intelligent.
3   https://www.historyofdatascience.com/
ai-winter-the-highs-and-lows-of-artificial-intelligence.
4   https://www.ibm.com/watson.
5   https://www.theguardian.com/technology/2011/feb/17/
ibm-computer-watson-wins-jeopardy.
6   https://deepmind.google/technologies/alphago/.
7   https://www.wired.com/2016/03/
two-moves-alphago-lee-sedol-redefined-future/.
8   https://www.zdnet.com/article/what-is-chatgpt-and-why-does-it-
matter-heres-everything-you-need-to-know.
9   https://chat.openai.com/.
10 https://www.theguardian.com/commentisfree/2022/dec/08/
the-guardian-view-on-chatgpt-an-eerily-good-human-impersonator.
11 https://www.cnet.com/tech/computing/
why-were-all-obsessed-with-the-mind-blowing-chatgpt-ai-chatbot.
12 Ibid.
13 https://www.ft.com/content/86e64b4c-a754-47d6-999c-fcc54f62fb5d.
14 https://kozyrkov.medium.com/.
15 https://finance.yahoo.com/news/chatgpt-gained-1-million-
followers-224523258.html.
16 https://techcrunch.com/2022/12/09/
is-chatgpt-a-virus-that-has-been-released-into-the-wild.

Chapter 7

1   https://www.forbes.com/sites/blakemorgan/2019/07/21/7-examples-
of-how-digital-transformation-impacted-business-performance.
2   https://www.computerweekly.com/news/252490791/
Pace-of-digital-transformation-accelerates.
3   https://en.wikipedia.org/wiki/Roy_Amara.
4   https://www.forbes.com/sites/forbesbusinesscouncil/2021/09/23/
why-the-era-of-digital-transformation-is-important-for-companies-of-
all-sizes.
5   https://www.mckinsey.com/capabilities/mckinsey-digital/our-insights/
strategy-for-a-digital-world.
6   Ibid.
7   https://www.earley.com/insights/knowledge/articles/
digital-transformation-staying-competitive.
8   https://www.sciencedirect.com/science/article/pii/
S0040162522008125.

9 https://hbr.org/insight-center/
how-digital-business-models-are-changing.
10 https://www.weforum.org/agenda/2021/10/
digital-transformation-business-resilience-cyber.
11 https://www.mckinsey.com/capabilities/mckinsey-digital/our-insights/
the-top-trends-in-tech.
12 Ibid.
13 https://en.wikipedia.org/wiki/World_Wide_Web.
14 https://www.theguardian.com/technology/2023/feb/02/
chatgpt-100-million-users-open-ai-fastest-growing-app.
15 https://chatnode.ai.
16 https://www.ibm.com/blog/watsonx-tailored-generative-ai/.

Chapter 8

1 https://www.unesco.org/en/digital-education/need-know.
2 https://www.technologyreview.com/2023/04/06/1071059/
chatgpt-change-not-destroy-education-openai.
3 https://www.cam.ac.uk/stories/ChatGPT-and-education.
4 https://www.unesco.org/en/articles/
turning-point-why-we-must-transform-education-now.
5 https://sites.psu.edu/mccormickcivicissues/2022/02/04/
the-positive-effects-of-covid-19-on-education/.
6 https://www.weforum.org/agenda/2022/11/
covid19-education-impact-legacy.
7 https://www.nature.com/articles/s41562-022-01506-4.
8 https://www.bbc.co.uk/news/education-60683839.
9 https://www.timeshighereducation.com/campus/
six-ingredients-successful-digital-transformation.
10 https://link.springer.com/
referenceworkentry/10.1007/978-3-030-10576-1_248.
11 https://en.wikipedia.org/wiki/Massive_open_online_course.
12 https://theconversation.com/the-russian-invasion-shows-how-digital-
technologies-have-become-involved-in-all-aspects-of-war-179918.
13 https://www.nationaldefensemagazine.org/articles/2023/3/24/
ukraine-a-living-lab-for-ai-warfare.
14 https://www.csis.org/analysis/
software-defined-warfare-architecting-dods-transition-digital-age.
15 https://www.ibm.com/blogs/think/uk-en/digital-transformation-in-
defence-balancing-the-strategic-and-the-tactical.
16 https://www.gov.uk/government/publications/
digital-strategy-for-defence-delivering-the-digital-

backbone-and-unleashing-the-power-of-defences-data/
digital-strategy-for-defence.

17 https://en.wikipedia.org/wiki/OODA_loop.

18 https://en.wikipedia.org/wiki/Kill_chain.

19 Brose, Christian. 2020. *The Kill Chain: Defending America in the Future of High-Tech Warfare.* Hachette.

20 Gasiorkiewicz, Lech, and Jan Monkiewicz (eds). 2022. *Digital Finance and the Future of the Global Financial System: Disruption and Innovation in Financial Services.* Routledge.

21 https://impact.economist.com/perspectives/financial-services/forging-new-frontiers-advanced-technologies-will-revolutionise-banking.

22 https://www.businessinsider.com/goldman-sachs-marcus-using-ai-powered-chatbots-manage-growth-2022-3.

23 https://assets.teradata.com/resourceCenter/downloads/CaseStudies/CaseStudy_EB9821_Danske_Bank_Fights_Fraud.pdf.

24 Townson, Sian. 2020. AI can make bank loans more fair. *Harvard Business Review*, November (https://hbr.org/2020/11/ai-can-make-bank-loans-more-fair).

25 https://thefinancialbrand.com/news/admin/feature/4-ways-personalization-is-evolving-at-top-banks-174569/.

26 https://www.fstech.co.uk/fst/HSBC_Card_Spend_Soars_15pc_After_AI_Rollout.php.

27 https://www.infosys.com/iki/perspectives/anti-money-laundering.html.

28 https://www.mckinsey.com/industries/financial-services/our-insights/capturing-the-full-value-of-generative-ai-in-banking.

29 https://www.cnbc.com/2023/03/22/goldman-sachs-experiments-with-chatgpt-like-ai-to-help-devs-write-code.html.

30 https://www.bloomberg.com/news/articles/2023-10-27/citi-charts-path-for-thousands-of-coders-to-experiment-with-ai.

31 https://www.mckinsey.com/industries/financial-services/our-insights/scaling-gen-ai-in-banking-choosing-the-best-operating-model.

32 https://www.accenture.com/gb-en/insights/banking/generative-ai-banking.

33 Davenport, Thomas, and George Westerman 2024. Case study: how aggressively should a bank pursue AI? *Harvard Business Review*, May (https://hbr.org/2024/05/case-study-how-aggressively-should-a-bank-pursue-ai).

34 https://www.ukfinance.org.uk/news-and-insight/press-release/majority-banks-are-piloting-opportunities-generative-ai-and.

35 https://www.forbes.com/sites/peterhigh/2024/01/10/
marsh-mclennan-cio-identifies-a-fast-track-to-drive-genai-value/.

36 https://www.bankofengland.co.uk/prudential-regulation/
publication/2022/october/artificial-intelligence.

37 https://www.theguardian.com/technology/2019/mar/17/the-
cambridge-analytica-scandal-changed-the-world-but-it-didnt-change-
facebook.

38 https://committees.parliament.uk/publications/2847/
documents/27859/default/.

39 Tapscott, Don. 1997. The Digital Economy: Promise and Peril in the Age
of Networked Intelligence. McGraw-Hill.

40 https://en.wikipedia.org/wiki/
Facebook%E2%80%93Cambridge_Analytica_data_scandal.

41 https://www.businessinsider.com/cambridge-analytica-a-guide-to-
the-trump-linked-data-firm-that-harvested-50-million-facebook-
profiles-2018-3?r=US&IR=T.

42 https://committees.parliament.uk/publications/2847/
documents/27859/default/.

43 https://www.newstatesman.com/long-reads/2020/10/
how-cambridge-analytica-scandal-unravelled.

44 https://www.newsweek.com/
netflix-cambridge-analytica-great-hack-brittany-kaiser-1451847.

Chapter 9

1 https://www.accenture.com/us-en/insights/artificial-intelligence/
responsible-ai-principles-practice.

2 https://www.theverge.com/features/23764584/ai-artificial-
intelligence-data-notation-labor-scale-surge-remotasks-openai-
chatbots.

3 https://stratechery.com/2021/
the-death-and-birth-of-technological-revolutions.

4 Obschonka, Martin. 2018. The Industrial Revolution left psychological
scars that can still be seen today. Harvard Business Review, March
(https://hbr.org/2018/03/research-the-industrial-revolution-left-
psychological-scars-that-can-still-be-seen-today).

5 Sanders, Nada, and John Wood. 2020. The secret to AI is people.
Harvard Business Review, August (https://hbr.org/2020/08/
the-secret-to-ai-is-people).

6 https://www.weforum.org/agenda/2023/05/jobs-lost-created-ai-gpt.

7 https://theconversation.com/ai-will-increase-inequality-and-raise-
tough-questions-about-humanity-economists-warn-203056.

8   https://www.brookings.edu/articles/
    protecting-privacy-in-an-ai-driven-world.
9   https://www.ieee.org/content/dam/ieee-org/ieee/web/org/about/
    european-public-policy/ethical-dilemmas-in-ai.pdf.
10 https://www.technologyreview.com/2018/10/24/139313/a-global-
    ethics-study-aims-to-help-ai-solve-the-self-driving-trolley-problem.
11 https://bpr.studentorg.berkeley.edu/2020/11/15/
    artificial-intelligence-and-the-loss-of-humanity.
12 https://www.nature.com/articles/d41586-020-00296-x.
13 https://www.theatlantic.com/magazine/archive/2008/07/
    is-google-making-us-stupid/306868/.
14 https://www.ibm.com/topics/explainable-ai.
15 https://www.economist.com/business/2023/08/13/
    ai-is-setting-off-a-great-scramble-for-data.
16 https://www.technologyreview.com/2020/11/18/1012234/training-
    machine-learning-broken-real-world-heath-nlp-computer-vision.
17 https://www.forbes.com/sites/forbestechcouncil/2022/06/27/
    training-data-the-overlooked-problem-of-modern-ai.
18 https://www.forbes.com/sites/nishatalagala/2022/03/02/data-as-the-
    new-oil-is-not-enough-four-principles-for-avoiding-data-fires.
19 https://www.ibm.com/blog/
    your-datas-been-prepared-now-train-the-ai-model.
20 https://www.technologyreview.com/2020/11/18/1012234/training-
    machine-learning-broken-real-world-heath-nlp-computer-vision.
21 https://en.wikipedia.org/wiki/Supervised_learning.
22 https://www.shaip.com/blog/the-true-cost-of-ai-training-data.
23 https://www.economist.com/technology-quarterly/2020/06/11/
    for-ai-data-are-harder-to-come-by-than-you-think.
24 https://www.npr.org/2023/06/26/1184392406/behind-the-secretive-
    work-of-the-many-many-humans-helping-to-train-ai.
25 https://www.techradar.com/news/chatgpt-explained.
26 https://blogs.ischool.berkeley.edu/w231/2021/06/18/
    ai-bias-where-does-it-come-from-and-what-can-we-do-about-it.
27 https://www.csis.org/blogs/strategic-technologies-blog/
    problem-bias-facial-recognition.
28 https://venturebeat.com/business/mit-study-finds-systematic-
    labeling-errors-in-popular-ai-benchmark-datasets.
29 https://towardsdatascience.com/understanding-noisy-data-and-
    uncertainty-in-machine-learning-4a2995a84198.
30 https://towardsdatascience.com/
    an-introduction-to-classification-using-mislabeled-data-581a6c09f9f5.

31 https://www.reuters.com/technology/who-warns-against-bias-misinformation-using-ai-healthcare-2023-05-16.

32 https://blog.re-work.co/how-to-scale-training-data-for-ai.

33 https://www2.deloitte.com/us/en/insights/industry/technology/ai-and-data-management.html.

34 https://knowledge.wharton.upenn.edu/article/big-data-ai-bias.

35 https://link.springer.com/article/10.1007/s40031-022-00713-x.

36 https://builtin.com/data-science/transfer-learning.

37 https://www.europarl.europa.eu/news/en/press-room/20240308IPR19015/artificial-intelligence-act-meps-adopt-landmark-law.

38 https://time.com/6903563/eu-ai-act-law-aritificial-intelligence-passes/.

39 https://www.ey.com/en_ch/forensic-integrity-services/the-eu-ai-act-what-it-means-for-your-business.

40 https://www.europarl.europa.eu/topics/en/article/20230601STO93804/eu-ai-act-first-regulation-on-artificial-intelligence.

41 https://www.chathamhouse.org/2024/03/eus-new-ai-act-could-have-global-impact.

42 https://www.weforum.org/agenda/2021/07/ai-machine-learning-bias-discrimination.

43 https://www.weforum.org/agenda/2021/01/how-to-address-artificial-intelligence-fairness.

44 https://www.economist.com/business/2023/03/26/big-tech-and-the-pursuit-of-ai-dominance.

45 https://www.nao.org.uk/reports/use-of-artificial-intelligence-in-government/.

46 https://www.nao.org.uk/insights/the-challenges-in-implementing-digital-change/.

47 https://www.ibm.com/watson/resources/ai-adoption.

48 https://www.microsoft.com/en-gb/ai/responsible-ai.

49 https://cloud.google.com/responsible-ai.

50 https://www.ibm.com/impact/ai-ethics.

51 https://www.bbc.co.uk/rd/publications/responsible-ai-at-the-bbc-our-machine-learning-engine-principles.

52 https://transform.england.nhs.uk/ai-lab/ai-lab-programmes/ethics.

53 https://www.gov.uk/government/publications/ambitious-safe-responsible-our-approach-to-the-delivery-of-ai-enabled-capability-in-defence.

Chapter 10

1 Schaffer, Robert H. 2017. All management is change management. *Harvard Business Review*, October (https://hbr.org/2017/10/all-management-is-change-management).
2 https://www.kotterinc.com/methodology/8-steps.
3 https://www.ukauthority.com/articles/making-tax-digital-now-at-five-times-original-cost.
4 https://www.oxfordreference.com/display/10.1093/acref/9780191826719.001.0001/q-oro-ed4-00007547.
5 https://www.weforum.org/agenda/2021/02/converting-digital-risk-into-opportunity-in-the-covid-19-era.
6 https://www.mckinsey.com/featured-insights/themes/how-to-build-digital-resilience.
7 https://www.mckinsey.com/capabilities/quantumblack/our-insights/exploring-opportunities-in-the-generative-ai-value-chain.
8 https://www.forbes.com/sites/quora/2019/11/15/what-exactly-is-machine-intelligence/.
9 https://www.surrey.ac.uk/sites/default/files/2018-11/machine-intelligence-report.pdf.
10 https://www.gov.uk/government/publications/digital-resilience-framework.

Chapter 11

1 https://www.drucker.institute/perspective/about-peter-drucker/.
2 Drucker, Peter. 2007. *Management Challenges for the 21st Century*. Routledge.
3 https://www.theguardian.com/books/2021/mar/21/values-by-mark-carney-review-call-for-a-new-kind-of-economics.
4 https://www.mckinsey.com/capabilities/strategy-and-corporate-finance/our-insights/how-big-companies-can-innovate.
5 https://www.mckinsey.com/capabilities/strategy-and-corporate-finance/our-insights/creating-an-innovation-culture.
6 Brynjolfsson, Erik, and Andrew McAfee. 2016. *The Second Machine Age: Work, Progress, and Prosperity in a Time of Brilliant Technologies*. W. W. Norton & Company.
7 Perez, Carlota. 2003. *Technological Revolutions and Financial Capital: The Dynamics of Bubbles and Golden Ages*. Edward Elgar.

8   https://www.mckinsey.com/business-functions/operations/our-insights/innovation-through-the-digital-disruption-of-customer-service.

9   https://www.nasa.gov/directorates/heo/scan/engineering/technology/technology_readiness_level.

10 https://blog.hubspot.com/service/customer-behavior-analysis.

11 https://www.inc.com/wanda-thibodeaux/this-tech-company-brought-in-anthropologists-to-work-with-its-designers-heres-why.html.

12 https://www2.deloitte.com/ch/en/pages/innovation/articles/platform-business-model-explained.html.

Chapter 12

1   https://variety.com/2017/digital/news/netflix-company-culture-document-1202474529.

2   https://www.atlassian.com/agile/agile-at-scale/spotify.

3   https://www.agilealliance.org/resources/experience-reports/when-moving-to-a-flat-agile-structure-understanding-what-drives-people-is-key.

4   https://www.scribd.com/document/412436980/Accenture-Strategy-Adapt-to-Survive-POV.

5   https://www.scrum.org/resources/blog/about-self-organizing-teams.

6   https://www.forbes.com/sites/stevedenning/2019/09/08/the-five-biggest-challenges-facing-agile.

7   https://www.pmi.org/learning/library/agile-problems-challenges-failures-5869.

8   https://www.oecd-forum.org/rooms/covid-19-the-great-digital-acceleration.

9   https://www.mckinsey.com/capabilities/strategy-and-corporate-finance/our-insights/how-covid-19-has-pushed-companies-over-the-technology-tipping-point-and-transformed-business-forever.

10 https://www.corporatecomplianceinsights.com/compliance-risks-covid-19-technology-adoption.

11 https://managedagile.com/topics/agile-leadership.

12 https://www.ibm.com/thought-leadership/institute-business-value/report/covid-19-future-business.

13 https://www.imd.org/research-knowledge/leadership/reports/redefining-leadership/.

14 https://sloanreview.mit.edu/projects/leaderships-digital-transformation.

15 https://www.forbes.com/sites/stevedenning.

16 https://www.wired.com/insights/2014/10/meritocracy.

17 https://www.datanami.com/2020/04/27/
    how-the-lack-of-good-data-is-hampering-the-covid-19-response.

18 Birkinshaw, Julian, and Jonas Ridderstrale. 2017. *Fast/Forward: Make Your Company Fit for the Future.* Stanford Business Books.

19 https://www.technologyreview.com/2024/01/04/1086046/
    whats-next-for-ai-in-2024/.

20 https://www.zdnet.com/article/best-ai-art-generator/.

21 http://www.eng.cam.ac.uk/news/
    quiet-ai-revolution-weather-forecasting.

22 https://www.theguardian.com/world/2024/jan/09/in-the-race-for-
    ai-supremacy-china-and-the-us-are-travelling-on-entirely-different-
    tracks.

23 https://www.washingtonpost.com/technology/2023/11/17/
    biden-xi-ai-china-us-apec/.

24 https://www.economist.com/china/2023/04/18/
    can-xi-jinping-control-ai-without-crushing-it.

25 https://thediplomat.com/2023/03/
    artificial-intelligence-will-bring-social-changes-in-china/.

26 https://www.theguardian.com/world/2023/mar/02/china-leading-us-
    in-technology-race-in-all-but-a-few-fields-thinktank-finds.

27 https://thediplomat.com/2022/08/
    why-ai-is-the-new-frontier-in-china-us-competition/.

28 https://www.forbes.com/sites/forbeseq/2023/07/18/how-does-chinas-
    approach-to-ai-regulation-differ-from-the-us-and-eu/.

29 https://www.journalofdemocracy.org/articles/
    how-ai-threatens-democracy/.

30 https://www.theguardian.com/technology/2020/mar/21/catherine-
    dignazio-data-is-never-a-raw-truthful-input-and-it-is-never-neutral.

31 https://www.technologyreview.com/2022/04/19/1049378/
    ai-inequality-problem/.

32 https://en.wikipedia.org/wiki/
    Facebook%E2%80%93Cambridge_Analytica_data_scandal.

33 https://journals.sagepub.com/doi/full/10.1177/20539517211029322.

34 https://d3.harvard.edu/
    james-mickens-on-why-all-data-science-is-political/.

35 https://journals.sagepub.com/doi/full/10.1177/2053951719885967.

36 https://www.forbes.com/sites/neilsahota/2024/01/12/
    the-ai-factor-in-political-campaigns-revolutionizing-modern-politics/.

37 Möhlmann, Mareike. 2021. Algorithmic nudges don't have to be
    unethical. *Harvard Business Review*, April (https://hbr.org/2021/04/
    algorithmic-nudges-dont-have-to-be-unethical).

38 https://www.unesco.org/en/artificial-intelligence/
recommendation-ethics.

39 https://www.ncbi.nlm.nih.gov/pmc/articles/PMC8826344/.

40 https://www.forbes.com/sites/
forbescommunicationscouncil/2022/08/17/
the-role-of-ethics-in-the-evolving-world-of-marketing-ai/.

41 https://www.ft.com/content/16f23c01-fa51-408e-acf5-0d30a5a1ebf2.

42 Simons, Josh. 2023. *Algorithms for the People: Democracy in the Age of
AI*. Princeton University Press.

43 Veliz, Carisa. 2021. *Privacy is Power: Why and How You Should Take Back
Control of Your Data*. Corgi.

Chapter 13

1 https://www.mckinsey.com/~/media/mckinsey/
business functions/quantumblack/our insights/
the state of ai in 2023 generative ais breakout year/
the-state-of-ai-in-2023-generative-ais-breakout-year_vf.pdf.

2 https://www.investopedia.com/
ai-is-the-biggest-tech-investing-theme-for-2024-8404597.

3 https://www.scientificamerican.com/article/
ai-anxiety-is-on-the-rise-heres-how-to-manage-it/.

4 https://www.itu.int/hub/2023/07/
a-call-to-action-for-inclusive-safe-and-responsible-ai/.

5 https://theconversation.com/researchers-warn-we-could-run-out-of-
data-to-train-ai-by-2026-what-then-216741.

6 https://www.forbes.com/sites/forbestechcouncil/2023/12/12/
thoughts-on-consent-and-privacy-in-the-age-of-ai/.

7 https://www.wired.co.uk/article/
uk-police-face-recognition-expansion.

8 https://www.cleanairfund.org/news-item/
ai-wearables-innovative-tech/.

9 https://www.insight.tech/cities/
ai-traffic-management-the-road-to-sustainable-smart-cities.

10 https://www.theguardian.com/uk-news/2023/oct/29/
britain-omni-surveillance-society-watchdog-warns.

11 https://www.technologyreview.com/2023/05/02/1072556/
we-need-to-bring-consent-to-ai/.

12 https://www.gov.uk/government/statistics/public-awareness-
opinions-and-expectations-about-artificial-intelligence-july-to-
october-2023.

13 https://medicalxpress.com/news/2023-11-consent-personal-health-
standardized-approach.html.

14 https://theweek.com/news/science-health/961529/
the-nhs-at-75-how-it-could-change-to-make-it-to-100.
15 https://papers.ssrn.com/sol3/papers.cfm?abstract_id=4626179.
16 https://www.nature.com/articles/5201117.
17 https://www.hrmagazine.co.uk/content/features/
four-lessons-on-ethical-ai-use-in-recruitment.
18 https://www.weforum.org/agenda/2023/12/
europe-landmark-ai-regulation-deal/.
19 https://oecd.ai/en/wonk/the-ai-data-challenge-how-do-we-protect-
privacy-and-other-fundamental-rights-in-an-ai-driven-world.
20 https://www.forbes.com/sites/forbesbusinesscouncil/2023/07/10/
how-ai-and-automation-are-transforming-the-world/.
21 https://www.theguardian.com/technology/2023/feb/08/
ai-chatgpt-jobs-economy-inequality.
22 https://www.consultancy.uk/news/35290/
two-fifths-of-professional-services-work-could-be-automated-with-ai.
23 https://technologymagazine.com/articles/
self-driving-trucks-leading-the-way-to-an-autonomous-future.
24 https://www.wired.com/story/workers-demand-job-security-in-the-
autonomous-electrified-future-of-transport/.
25 https://www.forbes.com/sites/johnhall/2023/02/24/
why-upskilling-and-reskilling-are-essential-in-2023/.
26 https://www.techradar.com/pro/the-ai-skills-gap-is-becoming-
incredibly-troubling-for-companies-everywhere.
27 https://www.investopedia.com/terms/b/basic-income.asp.
28 https://www.theguardian.com/society/2023/jun/04/universal-basic-
income-of-1600-pounds-a-month-to-be-trialled-in-england.
29 https://www.theguardian.com/global-development/2023/nov/16/ai-is-
coming-for-our-jobs-could-universal-basic-income-be-the-solution.
30 https://www.forbes.com/sites/forbesbusinesscouncil/2023/02/10/
the-importance-of-considering-collaboration-during-digital-
transformation/.
31 https://foreignpolicy.com/2023/05/29/
ai-regulation-global-south-artificial-intelligence/.
32 https://www.gov.uk/government/publications/
ai-safety-summit-2023-chairs-statement-2-november/
chairs-summary-of-the-ai-safety-summit-2023-bletchley-park.
33 Friis, Simon, and James Riley. 2023. Eliminating algorithmic
bias is just the beginning of equitable AI. *Harvard
Business Review*, September (https://hbr.org/2023/09/
eliminating-algorithmic-bias-is-just-the-beginning-of-equitable-ai).

34 https://theconversation.com/ai-can-reinforce-discrimination-but-used-correctly-it-could-make-hiring-more-inclusive-207966.

35 https://www.forbes.com/sites/forbestechcouncil/2023/09/25/ai-bias-in-recruitment-ethical-implications-and-transparency/.

36 https://www.forbes.com/sites/forbestechcouncil/2023/10/18/how-to-control-for-ai-bias-in-lending/.

37 https://www.forbes.com/sites/forbesfinancecouncil/2023/12/26/the-benefits-and-risks-of-ai-in-financial-services/.

38 https://www.nature.com/articles/s41598-023-36339-2.

39 https://policyreview.info/articles/analysis/navigating-ai-frontier-european-parliamentary-insights.

40 https://www.forbes.com/sites/forbestechcouncil/2023/03/10/15-key-mistakes-to-avoid-when-training-ai-models/.

41 https://dl.acm.org/doi/fullHtml/10.1145/3531146.3534644.

42 https://hbr.org/2023/05/ai-can-be-both-accurate-and-transparent.

43 https://kpmg.com/uk/en/blogs/home/posts/2023/12/which-way-now-keeping-ethical-approaches-at-the-heart-of-ai.html.

44 https://www.nature.com/articles/d41586-023-01689-4.

45 Ibid.

46 https://www.pewresearch.org/internet/2023/02/24/the-future-of-human-agency/.

47 https://www.theguardian.com/technology/2023/mar/29/elon-musk-joins-call-for-pause-in-creation-of-giant-ai-digital-minds.

48 https://www.nationaldefensemagazine.org/articles/2023/3/24/ukraine-a-living-lab-for-ai-warfare.

49 Ibid.

50 https://www.forbes.com/sites/davidhambling/2023/10/17/ukraines-ai-drones-seek-and-attack-russian-forces-without-human-oversight/.

51 https://www.npr.org/2023/08/05/1192343968/how-the-use-of-drones-in-ukraine-has-changed-war-as-we-know-it.

52 https://www.newscientist.com/article/2397389-ukrainian-ai-attack-drones-may-be-killing-without-human-oversight/.

53 https://www.mckinsey.com/capabilities/people-and-organizational-performance/our-insights/human-centered-ai-the-power-of-putting-people-first.

54 https://www.forbes.com/sites/forbestechcouncil/2023/01/13/explainable-ai-the-importance-of-adding-interpretability-into-machine-learning/.

55 Kendall Roundtree, Aimee. 2023. AI explainability, interpretability, fairness, and privacy: an integrative review of reviews. In *Artificial*

Intelligence in HCI, chapter 12. Springer (https://link.springer.com/chapter/10.1007/978-3-031-35891-3_19).

56 https://www.turing.ac.uk/research/research-projects/ai-ethics-and-governance-practice.

57 https://www.gartner.com/en/newsroom/press-releases/2023-07-27-gartner-survey-finds-55-of-organizations-that-have-deployed-ai-take-an-ai-first-strategy-with-new-use-cases.

58 https://www.nist.gov/itl/ai-risk-management-framework.

59 https://www.europarl.europa.eu/news/en/headlines/society/20230601STO93804/eu-ai-act-first-regulation-on-artificial-intelligence.

60 https://carnegieendowment.org/2023/07/10/china-s-ai-regulations-and-how-they-get-made-pub-90117.

61 https://www.whitehouse.gov/briefing-room/presidential-actions/2023/10/30/executive-order-on-the-safe-secure-and-trustworthy-development-and-use-of-artificial-intelligence/.

62 https://www.gov.uk/government/publications/ai-regulation-a-pro-innovation-approach.

63 https://www.computerworld.com/article/3705950/pew-research-finds-a-big-problem-with-ai-people-dont-trust-it.html.

64 https://journals.aom.org/doi/abs/10.5465/AMPROC.2023.10072symposium.

65 https://datahoarder.io/what-is-datahoarding/.

66 https://publiclawproject.org.uk/latest/government-behind-the-curve-on-ai-risks/.

67 https://theconversation.com/a-survey-of-over-17-000-people-indicates-only-half-of-us-are-willing-to-trust-ai-at-work-200256.

68 https://www.forbes.com/sites/joemckendrick/2022/03/29/resolving-artificial-intelligences-trust-problem/.

69 https://d.docs.live.net/7ee3b17125128abe/Documents/Dispatches-Book/AI is its growing role in generating misinformation and deep fakes.

70 https://www.forbes.com/sites/forbestechcouncil/2023/06/23/the-ethics-of-ai-navigating-bias-manipulation-and-beyond/.

71 https://www.technologyreview.com/2023/10/04/1080801/generative-ai-boosting-disinformation-and-propaganda-freedom-house/.

72 https://www.theguardian.com/technology/2023/may/20/elections-in-uk-and-us-at-risk-from-ai-driven-disinformation-say-experts.

73 https://www.theverge.com/2023/6/29/23778068/meta-facebook-instagram-social-media-algorithms-ai-transparency.

74 https://royalsociety.org/topics-policy/publications/2023/digital-content-provenance-bbc/.

75 https://sproutsocial.com/insights/social-media-algorithms/.
76 https://www.goldmansachs.com/intelligence/pages/the-generative-world-order-ai-geopolitics-and-power.html.
77 https://www.economist.com/business/2023/12/26/china-is-shoring-up-the-great-firewall-for-the-ai-age.
78 Taneja, Hemant, and Fareed Zakaria. 2023. AI and the new digital cold war. *Harvard Business Review*, September (https://hbr.org/2023/09/ai-and-the-new-digital-cold-war).
79 https://www.vox.com/technology/2023/7/27/23808499/ai-openai-google-meta-data-privacy-nope.
80 https://www.techtarget.com/whatis/feature/Tim-Berners-Lees-Solid-explained-What-you-need-to-know.
81 https://www.hubofallthings.com/.
82 https://arxiv.org/abs/2209.04053.
83 https://www.techrepublic.com/article/what-is-data-literacy/.
84 https://www.forbes.com/sites/forbestechcouncil/2023/08/15/shaping-the-ai-future-a-shared-journey/.
85 https://www.adalovelaceinstitute.org/evidence-review/what-do-the-public-think-about-ai/.

Chapter 14

1 https://www.zdnet.com/article/is-ai-the-biggest-bubble-of-all-time-stability-ai-ceo-thinks-so/.
2 https://www.businessinsider.com/ai-hype-could-end-up-like-dot-com-bubble-investor-2023-6?op=1.
3 https://cmte.ieee.org/futuredirections/2023/08/22/is-ai-really-great-or-just-another-bubble/.
4 https://techcrunch.com/2023/12/14/openai-thinks-superhuman-ai-is-coming-and-wants-to-build-tools-to-control-it/.
5 https://www.forbes.com/sites/ashleystahl/2022/05/03/the-rise-of-artificial-intelligence-will-robots-actually-replace-people/.
6 https://www.wired.com/story/get-ready-for-the-great-ai-disappointment/.
7 https://www.mckinsey.com/capabilities/mckinsey-digital/our-insights/tech-forward/scaling-ai-for-success-four-technical-enablers-for-sustained-impact.
8 https://doctorow.medium.com/what-kind-of-bubble-is-ai-d02040b5573a.
9 https://huggingface.co/.
10 https://llama.meta.com/.
11 https://pytorch.org/.

12 https://www.tensorflow.org/.

Chapter 15

1 https://www.mckinsey.com/capabilities/people-and-organizational-performance/our-insights/the-organization-of-the-future-enabled-by-gen-ai-driven-by-people.

2 https://www.turing.ac.uk/news/ai-could-help-automate-around-84-repetitive-service-transactions-across-government.

3 https://techmonitor.ai/government-computing/automation-ai-jobs-cuts-civil-service-mid-2030s-former-chro-rupert-mcneil.

4 Ambler, Scott, and Mark Lines. 2012. *Disciplined Agile Delivery: A Practitioner's Guide to Agile Software Delivery in the Enterprise*. IBM Press.

5 Rigby, Darrel, Jeff Sutherland and Andy Noble. 2018. Agile at scale. *Harvard Business Review*, May (https://hbr.org/2018/05/agile-at-scale).

6 https://www.forbes.com/sites/forbesbusinesscouncil/2023/10/24/11-challenges-of-adopting-ai-in-business-and-how-to-address-them-head-on/.

7 https://www.forbes.com/sites/forbestechcouncil/2021/04/01/five-barriers-to-digital-transformation-and-how-to-overcome-them/?sh=714e7921b112.

8 https://www.businesstechweekly.com/operational-efficiency/artificial-intelligence/barriers-to-ai-adoption/.

9 https://www.mckinsey.com/capabilities/mckinsey-digital/our-insights/rewired-and-running-ahead-digital-and-ai-leaders-are-leaving-the-rest-behind.

10 https://digileaders.com/.

11 https://digileaders.kartra.com/page/ai-survey-free-download.

12 https://www.nao.org.uk/reports/use-of-artificial-intelligence-in-government/.

13 https://www.civilserviceworld.com/professions/article/ai-only-sustainable-route-to-cutting-civil-service-headcount-dowden-claims.

14 https://www.globalgovernmentforum.com/uks-deputy-prime-minister-says-ai-key-to-transform-productivity-of-the-civil-service/.

15 https://www.gov.uk/government/publications/national-ai-strategy.

16 https://www.techuk.org/resource/uk-government-doubles-down-efforts-to-deploy-ai-across-the-public-sector.html.

17 https://www.nao.org.uk/insights/the-challenges-in-implementing-digital-change/.